Tableau 10

For Beginners

Version 10.x

Chandraish Sinha

Copyright © 2017

www.OhioComputerAcademy.com

Legal Notes

About The Author

Chandraish Sinha has 19 years of experience in implementing Business Intelligence solutions. His experience involves working in different BI applications. He has worked in multiple Tableau end-to-end implementations.

He coaches organizations and consultants in exploring the visualization world of Tableau.

He has a passion for Tableau and shares his knowledge through his blog (http://www.learntableaupublic.com/).

Other books by the author:

1. Tableau Dashboards: Step by Step guide to developing visualizations in Tableau 9.2
2. Tableau Questions & Answers: Guide to Tableau concepts and FAQs
3. QlikView Essentials
4. QlikView Questions and Answers: Guide to QlikView and FAQs
5. How to be a Successful IT Professional in the USA: A Checklist and Easy Guide to Success

Word from the Author

Thank you for providing great support to my earlier book
Tableau Dashboards: Step by Step guide to developing visualizations in Tableau 9.2

My objective with this new book is to explain all the Tableau 10 concepts in a simple, easy-to-understand manner.

In this book, I have tried my best to cover the feedbacks received on my earlier work.

As always, please do write to me at chandraish@gmail.com. I personally read and respond to all my messages.

New in this book:
1. Sample workbooks available on Tableau public
2. Tableau concepts as per version 10.1
3. Types of Files in Tableau
4. Analytics pane
5. Explanation of Discrete and Continuous concept
6. How dates work in Tableau
7. Nested Sort
8. New chapter on Formatting
9. New visualizations/Charts
10. Creating custom color palettes
11. Creating custom territories in Maps
12. New Chapter on Server Deployment

New in Tableau 10 Desktop
1. Enhanced look and feel of Tableau desktop.
2. Cross-table joins. See Chapter 2-Connecting to data source.
3. Clustering. See Chapter 11 – Visualization.
4. Building custom territory in Maps. See Chapter 10 – Creating Maps.
5. New highlighter feature. See Chapter 9 – Formatting.
6. Device preview for dashboards. See Chapter 12 – Dashboards and Visual Story.

Contents

Preface

Tableau provides an innovative way to look at the data. The popularity of Tableau is due to the fact that Tableau can extract huge amounts of data and present it in a format that is easy to understand and interpret.

The objective of this book is to help readers understand and practice Tableau concepts.

This book offers detailed explanation of key concepts in Tableau. It explains each concept in a very easy-to-understand manner. Every topic is explained and followed by step-by-step exercises. It provides direction and guidance for advanced exploration.

About this book

Chapter1. Understanding the Basics

This Chapter provides an overview of BI and Tableau concepts.

Chapter2. Connecting to Data

In this chapter, we can learn about creating data connections. This chapter also provides details on different features of Tableau desktop. In this chapter, you can create your first Tableau workbook. It will give a peek into different concepts in Tableau visualization.

Chapter3. Data Transformation

This chapter talks about data preparation for creating useful visualization. Learn about data blending, creating hierarchy and organizing data elements.

Chapter4. Creating Calculations

This chapter explains how to create calculated fields in Tableau. It also provides details on Table calculations and LODs.

Chapter5. More Calculations

This chapter contains more calculation types like Number, string and date.

Chapter6. Filters and Parameters

This chapter contains filters and parameters as used in Tableau.

Chapter7. Sorting

This chapter shows how sorting works in Tableau - Manual and Calculated.

Chapter8. Groups and Sets

Learn about creating Groups and Sets in this chapter.

Chapter9. Formatting

In this chapter learn about all the formatting options available in Tableau to enhance an application.

Chapter10. Creating Maps

This chapter deals with displaying data according to the geographical locations.

Chapter11. Creating Visualizations

In this chapter learn about creating different types of charts.

Chapter12. Dashboards and visual Story

Learn how to create dashboards and story in Tableau.

Chapter13. Server Deployment

This chapter shows how to deploy data sources and visualization on Tableau server.

How to use this Book

In this book, every chapter starts with concepts followed by step-by-step exercises. Go through each concept and practice the exercises.

To recreate scenarios presented in this book, download **Tableau desktop or Tableau Public**.

These applications can be downloaded for free from
https://public.tableau.com/en-us/s/download

Tableau desktop trial version is available for two weeks. For students, Tableau provides one year of free license. The trial version allows you to use file based data sources such as Ms-Excel, Text or Access files. Connection to other data sources are only allowed with the licensed version.

Tableau Public can be used for free for unlimited period of time. Tableau Public has all the functionalities of Tableau desktop. Workbooks developed using Tableau Public are saved only to Tableau Public and are accessible to everyone.

Who needs this book?

This book provides all the Tableau concepts according to Tableau version 10. It also contains overview of deploying objects on the server.

This book is good for anyone starting career in Tableau. The book starts with basic data-warehousing concepts and covers all the concepts in-depth.

This book is also useful for experienced Tableau developers who want to explore additional charts and functionalities. This book should work as a guide and encouragement for further exploration.

Data used in the book

After Tableau desktop installation on your machine, locate folder **My Tableau Repository** under **My documents** folder. Under "My Tableau Repository", look for **Datasources** sub-folder. This folder contains all the Tableau provided data sources. Copy other data sources which comes with this book-in this folder.

- **Sample- Superstore.xls** this datasource comes with Tableau desktop installation. It contains 3 worksheets – Orders, Returns and People.
- **Shipper_Info_10.xls** this datasource contains Shipper info and is provided to show an example of how different datasources can be joined in Tableau.
- **Emp_Dept_10.mdb.** This database contains Employee, department and Salary tables. It is used to explain Joins.
- **SalesReport_10.xls** is also used in few examples. This excel is provided to explain data transformation.

Get data and Sample Workbooks

The book comes with 20+ sample workbooks.

All workbooks are present on Tableau Public. See the link at the beginning of the exercises.

Sample workbooks and data files can also be downloaded from http://www.learntableaupublic.com/. Look for the **Book Resource** tab on the main navigation.

Other Resources

http://www.tableau.com/ is a good resource for information. Visit http://www.tableau.com/learn/training for free online videos provided by Tableau.

Also visit Author's blog http://www.learntableaupublic.com/ for more tips, blogs and announcements.

1

Understanding the Basics

Tableau is an awesome visualization and dash boarding application. Tableau is a Business Intelligence application and is being utilized by 100's of business users to gain business insights.

Before embarking on the Tableau journey, let's learn some basics.

What is Business Intelligence (BI)

Business Intelligence or BI is a concept that deals with analysis of diverse data. BI uses different tools and technologies to help in gathering, transforming and presenting data. Presentation of data is such that it helps business users in understanding the data and arriving at meaningful decisions.

Some of the keywords used in explaining Business Intelligence are:

> Data Warehouse

Data warehouse is a large storage of enterprise data. It is used for the ease of reporting and analysis. It is usually derived from the relational database system.

> Data Mart

Data Mart is similar to data warehouse but smaller in nature. It pertains to a specific business area or department.

> Star schema

Star schema is designed for the ease in analytics. It contains dimensions and fact tables.

Fact tables contains measurable attribute of the data such as sales and revenue.

Dimensions contain the descriptive attribute of the data such as Product description and Customer info. A fact is surrounded by dimension tables.

In Star Schema, a fact table is surrounded by multiple Dimension tables. It looks like Star, hence the name.

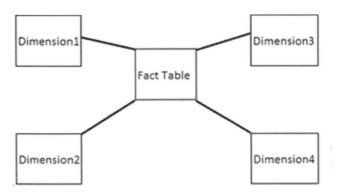

➤ Snow flake schema

In star schema, Dimension tables are connected to fact tables. Snow flake schema is similar to star schema with the only difference being, a dimension table can connect to another dimension table.

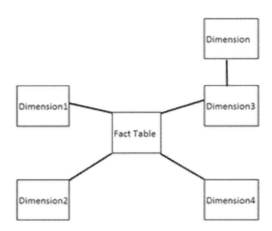

How Tableau Works

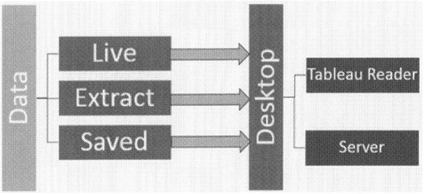

> ➤ Tableau can connect to any datasource. This data connection can be a **Live** connection or an **Extract**. It can also be a saved connection or a published connection.
> ➤ Tableau desktop is used to create workbooks. These workbooks use data connections to create charts and tables.
> ➤ Users view these dashboards using Tableau Reader or a server.

Overview of Tableau

Tableau's powerful visualizations help business users in gaining useful insights into their data.

- Tableau is a Business Intelligence application. It helps business in creating interactive visualization to gain data insights.
- Tableau can connect to any data source. Tableau uses the data at a granular level. Data is not pre-aggregated.
- When a measure is used in Tableau, it is automatically aggregated, by default it uses Sum. This aggregation type can be changed say from Sum to Average or Count.
- Components of Tableau are **Tableau desktop**, **Tableau Reader** and **Tableau Server/Publisher**.

- The developer uses Tableau desktop to create visualizations, dashboards and stories.
- Dashboards are deployed on the Tableau Server. The User can access dashboards through server url.
- Tableau desktop can use data as a "Live" connection or as an "Extract" **(TDE)**. Data connection/s used in developing dashboards are reusable. Data connections can be published to the server.
- Tableau desktop design file is called a "Workbook". It has an extension **.twb**.
- Tableau workbooks can also be packaged with data. This packaged workbook is a zip file with extension **.twbx**.
- In the absence of the server, Tableau design files can be viewed by using Tableau Reader. Tableau reader is available for free download and can open twbx files.
- **Tableau Public** is a free service provided by Tableau software that allows users to publish their dashboards on the Tableau public Server. All the content is owned by Tableau.
- **Tableau Online** is Tableau server on the cloud. Organizations can publish their dashboards on the cloud. Only authorized users can interact with the data and dashboards.

My Tableau Repository

When Tableau Desktop is installed, it creates a "**My Tableau Repository**" folder under "My Documents" folder.
My Repository folder contains all the files required for Tableau dashboard development.

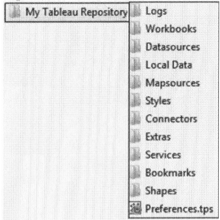

Some important folders in this location are:

- **Logs** - This folder contains all the issue logs.
- **Workbooks** - contains all the workbooks – twb and twbx files. Save all your workbooks in this folder.
- **Datasources -** this folder is used to keep all the datasource files such as csv, excel etc. Save all data sources provided with this book in this sub-folder.
- **Local Data -** when custom geocoding is imported, it gets stored in this folder.
- **Mapsources** - Tableau Map Source (.tms) file is stored in this folder.
- **Bookmarks –** Files with .tbm file extension are stored in this folder.
- **Shapes** - this folder contains all the shapes provided by Tableau. To add your custom shapes, copy custom shapes in an image format and add to a new folder under this folder.
- **Preference.tps** - file is used to add custom color palettes.

Types of Files in Tableau

Tableau has different kinds of files/extensions

TWB

Twb or Tableau Workbook contains worksheets, dashboards, Story and data souces. Twb file is created using Tableau desktop.

Users can view TWB files on Tableau desktop or Tableau Server.

To open a twb file, the user should have access to the twb file and the data source file or connection.

By default, a twb file is saved under your **My Tableau repository/Workbooks** folder.

TWBX

TWBX is a zip or packaged file which contains workbook and data source files used in the workbook.

Twbx contains all the information like background images, maps, worksheets and dashboards.

We can save a twb file as .twbx.

TWBX files can be viewed and opened using Tableau desktop, Tableau server and Tableau Reader.

By default, twbx file is saved under your **My Tableau repository/Workbooks** folder.

TDS

A TDS file contain the data source connection information and the transformations made to the metadata. The file does not have any data source, but contains all the information relating to the modifications made to the fields such as calculated Fields, default properties, groups and so on.

In Tableau desktop, connect to the data source and create the required transformations.

To create a TDS file, just right click on the datasource name and select **Add to saved data source**.

TDS files are reusable. Power users can use saved datasource / TDS files to create their own dashboards. Complexity of the data source will be hidden for them.

By default, TDS file is saved under your **My Tableau repository/Datasources** folder.

TDSX

A TDSX file contains all the information that a TDS file contains and in addition, it will also contain a **TDE/Tableau data extract file** . TDSX is zip file just like TWBX but, it will not have any worksheets or dashboards. It will contain the data connection information and be packaged with TDE data source file.

A TDSX file is saved similar to a TDS file. While saving the datasource, it will display both options.

The advantage of using a TDSX file is that it comes with the data so it can be used in offline mode.

By default, TDSX file is saved under your **My Tableau repository/Datasources** folder.

TDE

TDE or Tableau data extract is the data extract file which can import a subset of data by using filters or the complete snapshot of data.

The file contains a local copy of the data source. It can be a subset or the entire data.

The option to save data as TDE will be displayed, once the data is connected as **Extract** in Tableau desktop. The TDE file doesn't contain any information about worksheets or dashboards. It will only contain the underlying data. Connecting to TDE files is faster compared to the Live connection.

TBM

Bookmarks can be used to save the individual worksheet of a workbook. This sheet will include data connections, formatting, color coding, etc. We can import this worksheet into the other workbooks.

The major benefit with book marks is reusability.

In a team, if two or more developers are working on the same data, they can merge all the worksheets to create a single workbook.

Bookmarks include Data connection, visualizations and filters. It will not include parameters.

To save the file as a book mark, on Tableau Desktop, navigate to main menu- **Window > Bookmark > Create Bookmark** and save it as .tbm file.

By default, Bookmarks will be saved in your **My Tableau Repository/Bookmarks**.

If you don't save the bookmark in the default My Repository location, it will not show up , when you try to use it in Tableau desktop.

TMS

We save this type of file, when we load Tableau with images from WMS Server for plotting custom maps instead of default tableau maps.

To save the file as .tms file:

In Tableau desktop, navigate to main menu **Map > Background Images > WMS Server > WMS Server Connections > Export the images**.

Save the file in My Tableau Repository/Mapsources for sharing and future use.

TPS

Tableau provides multiple color palettes, but in case you have to create a custom color palette, use **Preferences.tps** file.

TPS file is used to create custom color palette for consistent colors across the organization.

Tableau provides the template of this file in My Tableau Repository folder, you will have to modify this file to create your custom colors.

2
Connecting to data

Tableau connects to a variety of data sources. Tableau connects to most of the data sources natively.

In this chapter, you will learn about data connections in Tableau.

You will connect to a file based datasource, learn more about Tableau desktop development environment and create your first sheet.

Data connection in Tableau

When Tableau desktop is launched, Data connection page is displayed. Tableau desktop personal edition provides access to only file based data sources such as Excel and Text files.

Licensed version of Tableau desktop allows connection to any data source. You can connect to new data, data on the server or saved data sources.

1. In Tableau, database tables and excel files work in a similar fashion. Individual worksheets in excel, work as database Tables. Data can be sourced from one or multiple sheets. Similar to tables, worksheets can be joined.

2. You can also connect to a different related datasource by creating a new connection. This new datasource can be a text file or a database table. Use **Add** option to add a new connection

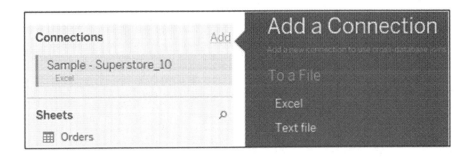

The table selected from this new data source can be joined to the tables from the existing datasource.

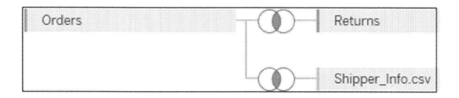

Data source can be connected as **Live** or **Extract**. If the extract option is selected, data is extracted into Tableau **TDE** files. Extracted data is a snapshot of the source and will need to be refreshed, if data in the underlying datasource changes. Extracts are faster as compared to live connection.

3. While creating data connection, a **Filter** can be applied to limit the data.

4. Data can also be transformed. You can change the **datatype**, **Rename** the fields, and **split** a composite field into multiple fields.

5. Some of the data sources have limits on whether they can be connected live or extract. For e.g. OLAP cube cannot be extracted and cloud data sources should always be extracted.

6. Data Sources can be saved and published on the server.

7. Data Source in the workbook can be refreshed. Right click on the data source and select **Refresh**.

8. Data sources can also be replaced with another data source.

    a. To replace an existing datasource, create a new data connection. Add a new datasource and in the data window, select **Replace Data Source**.

Download Sample workbook - http://tabsoft.co/2ppqz5w
Exercise - Connecting to the Datasource

In this exercise, we will connect to **Sample – Superstore.xls**
1. Launch Tableau desktop.
2. Click on **Excel** under **Connect**
3. Browse to **Sample – Superstore.xls** under the following path \My Tableau Repository\Datasources\10.1\en_US-US
4. The name of the datasource and sheets in xls will be visible. The Datasource name can be modified.

5. Drag **Orders** table/sheet to **Drag sheets here** space.

6. On the right most corner, make sure to select **Live** so that data is connected as live and not as an extract. Preview of the data is available. In the preview, only 1000 rows of data are visible.
7. Explore different options. You can change the datatype, rename the columns and so on.

❖ Once you have connected to the data, you will see more options.

Manage metadata option will provide a useful interface to change the datatype, rename the columns and so on

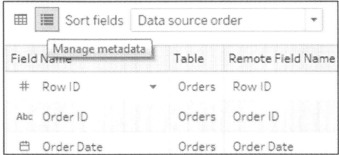

8. Click on **Go to Worksheet Sheet** or **Sheet 1** at the bottom of the screen to navigate to the development canvas of Tableau.

9. Tableau automatically segregate your data in Dimensions and Measures.
10. Save this workbook as **Chapter2-ConnectingtoData.twb** or as **twbx**.

❖ Twbx is a packaged workbook. It has data enclosed with it. In this book, twb and twbx will be used interchangeably, as user can save the workbook in either way.

Overview of Tableau Desktop

Tableau desktop is a development environment and provides functionality to develop interactive dashboards.

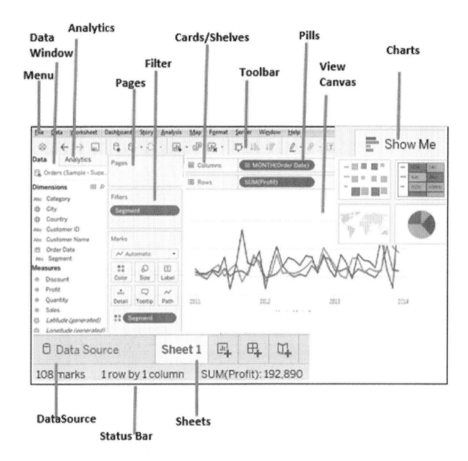

1. **Menu.** Menu is used to create a new file or save an existing file. It also performs other tasks such as creating new sheets, dashboards etc.

2. **Data window/pane.** Displays information about the data connection and fields in the data source. Fields in the tables are automatically divided into Dimensions and Measures.

3. **Analytics.** Contains ready-to use objects for faster analysis of data.
4. **Pages.** This shelf displays views into different pages. If a dimension is placed on Pages, it creates separate pages for each dimension. If a measure is used then the measure is converted to discrete measure.
5. **Filters.** Filter shelf is used to place filters that limit the data.
6. **Cards/shelves.** Views are created by placing fields on the cards or shelves. **Mark** has different cards such as color, size, label, detail, tooltip. Fields can be placed on these shelves. Changing the Mark type as Automatic, Shape will change these shelves.
7. **Toolbar.** Toolbar provides quick access to different functionalities such as undo/redo, adding sheets, sorting, displaying labels and so on.
8. **Pills.** Fields or calculations on the rows or columns are called Pills. Click on a pill to access pull down menu options such as filter, Table calculations etc. Dimension pill is **Blue** in color and Measure pill is **Green**.
9. **View/Canvas.** This space displays visualization created by the fields placed on the shelves.
10. **Show Me.** Depending on the field selection in the data window, Tableau suggests the best suited visualization. Different visualizations can be selected from the **Show Me** box.
11. **Status bar.** Displays various attributes of the visualization in the current worksheet. It displays information such as number of Marks, number of rows and columns and aggregated measure.

Analytics Pane

On the Tableau desktop, **Analytics** pane appears by the side of the Data pane. User can toggle between the Data pane and Analytics pane.

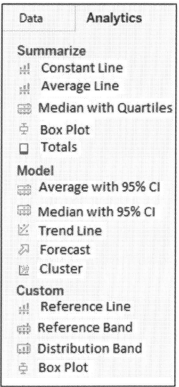

The Analytics pane provides easy-to-use functionality to Tableau's analytic features.

The functionality available in this pane, is also available in other places in the Tableau desktop; Analytics pane just provides drag-and-drop functionality to these features.

❖ See how to use the Analytics pane at the end of this chapter.

Visualization Basics

Visualization involves representing data visually using tools like graphs, tables and maps. This helps in faster understanding of the data.

A case of Discrete and Continuous

Before diving more into visualization, it is important to understand the concept of discrete and continuous.

In Tableau, when you connect to a data source, data is automatically segregated between **Dimensions** and **Measures**.

- ❖ Dimensions are descriptive attributes of the data, such as Region or Segment. Measures are measurable attributes of the data, such as Sales and Revenue.
- ❖ Dimensions provide context to the Measure. For example, Sales by Region. Dimensions help group the aggregated measure.

Dimensions are **discrete** and Measures are **Continuous**.
Discrete means unique categories of data.
For e.g., Region has four distinct values East, West, North and South.
Continuous means range of values. Sales can take up any value in a range of numeric values. It is not finite or unique like Region.
In Tableau, Dimension can be converted to continuous and Measure can be converted to discrete.

- ❖ When you hover over a Dimension or Measure field in the data pane, Dimensions/discrete data fields are displayed in blue and Measures/continuous data fields are displayed in green (see the picture below).

How visualization is built in Tableau

When a **Discrete** value is placed in the view, it creates **Labels** and when a **Continuous** value is placed in the view, it creates **Axis**.

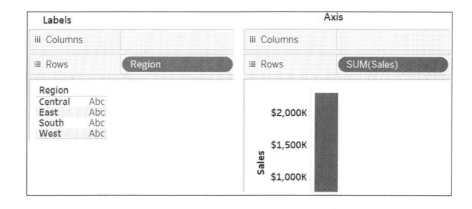

How Dates work in Tableau

Dates are essential for any dash boarding application.
In Tableau, Dates can be Discrete or Continuous. When data is loaded, Dates come automatically as a Dimension/Discrete value.
Tableau creates automatic hierarchy for dates, such as Year, Quarter, Months and so on.

Date Properties

Date properties can be set from the **Data** pane. Right click on the Data source and select **Date Properties**.

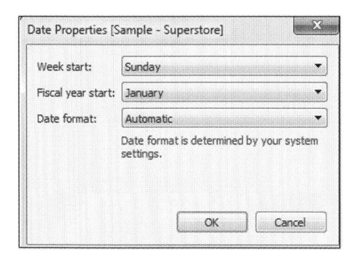

You can change these settings according to your Organization's requirement. If no changes are made, Tableau uses your system's local settings.

Discrete and Continuous Dates
Dates by default are treated as Dimensions/Discrete. Depending on the visualization requirements, you can convert date to Continuous.
There are two ways to convert a date to discrete or continuous,
1. In the Data pane, right-click on the Date field and select **Convert to Continuous**.

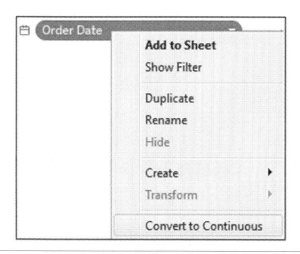

❖ Notice when Date is discrete, it is in blue color. Once it is converted to continuous, it changes to green color.

2. If the Date is used in the view, Columns or rows, click on the pill and choose the Discrete or continuous options.
In the picture below, the top box is for discrete date values and the bottom box is for the continuous date values. Based on your requirement, you can select either one.

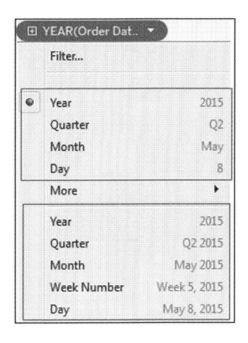

When Date is discrete, clicking on  next to the date, drills down and creates a field next in the hierarchy

When the date is Continuous, hierarchy is not present. There is no drill-down behavior, the next date field gets displayed.

Using visualizations to answer business questions

Visualizations help in answering business questions and making meaningful decisions.

Since visualizations help in answering different questions, the following exercises would be useful for the same.

Download Sample workbook - http://tabsoft.co/2ppD2Xf
Exercise

Question: Products are being sold for the past four years. What is the profit over time?

1. Launch Tableau desktop. Open Chapter2-ConnectingtoData and save as Chapter2-VisualizationBasics.

> a. From the Data window, double click on **Order Date** and **Profit**. Tableau will use best visualization practice and will create a Trend line or Bar chart. Make sure **Mark type** is set to **Automatic**. Mark Type can be changed to get any desired visualization.
>
> b. Rename this sheet as YearOverYear Trend.

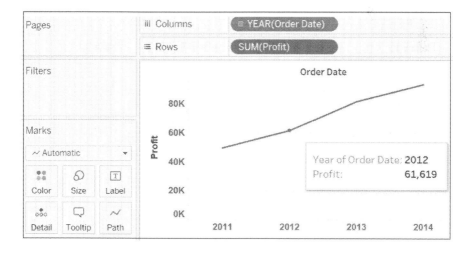

Question: How can you compare Quantity with the Profit earned?

a. Create a new sheet and name it **Charts**.

b. From the data window, double click on **Quantity** and **Profit**. You will get a chart with a circle. This type of Chart is called **Scatter chart**. This gives an overall Sum of Quantity and Profit for the entire data set. Notice Number of Mark on the status bar of the screen – 1 row by 1 column.

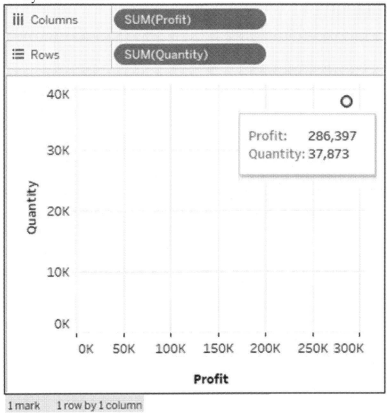

Tableau automatically creates an aggregation for the measure fields, which is by default their **Sum**. This aggregation can be changed by clicking on the pill for Sum (Profit) or Sum (Quantity)

Question. How do Profit and Quantity perform in each of the Regions?

> a. From the **Dimensions**, place **Region** to the **Color**. The Chart now displays Profit and Quantity by Regions. Notice Number of Mark on the status bar.

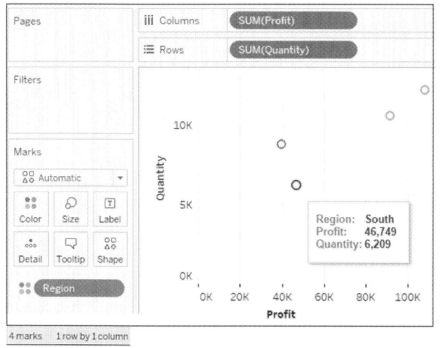

Question. How do Profit and Quantity perform per Region and per Segment?

> a. On the same chart, place **Segment** to **Shape**. The Chart displays Profit and Quantity for each Region and Segment. Notice how Mark has changed with the increase in data points.

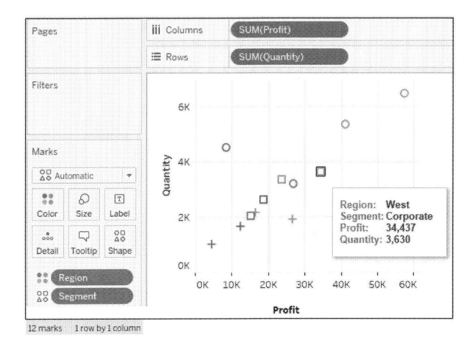

Region and Segment will be displayed as legends on the chart.

When you hover over a data point and don't see the details of the data points, click on **Tooltip** card and enter the respective data elements. You can select the specific data elements by selecting them from **Insert** drop down.

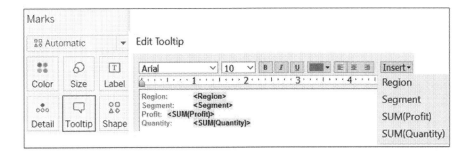

2. Granularity of the chart, can also be changed without bringing the field to the color or shape or size. This can be done by using **Detail**.

     a. Duplicate the Charts sheet and name the new sheet as "Details".

b. Place **Customer Name** on the **Detail**. This will change the granularity of the chart, without displaying Customer as color or shape.

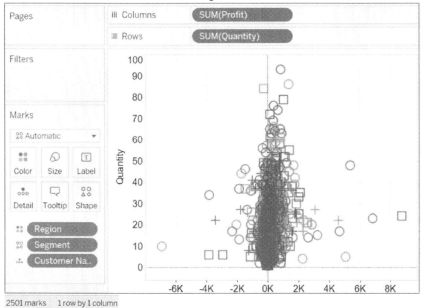

3. **Show Me**. Show Me feature guides the user in selecting the visualization best suited for the selected fields.

a. Create a new sheet and name it "Show Me".

b. On the data window, ctrl + click the fields **Region**, **Segment**, **Profit** and **Quantity**.

Open **Show Me** from the extreme right of the tool bar. The highlighted Chart is the suggestion made by Tableau based on the field selection. Click on the highlighted chart to get the desired chart on the view.

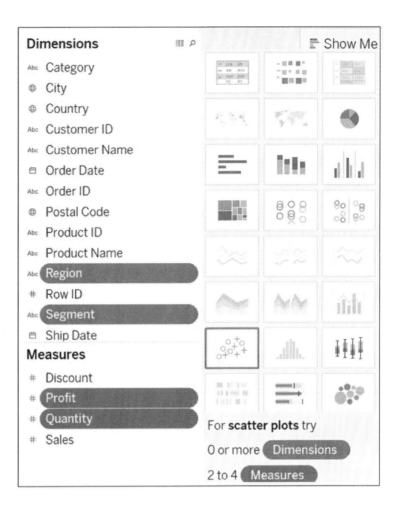

Drill Downs

In Tableau, drill down is allowed in the hierarchies present in the data. Some of the hierarchies are pre-built, for example, in the case of Year, Quarter, Month and so on. Other hierarchies can be created based on the data usage and requirements.

1. Use the above file Chapter2-VisualizationBasics. Create a new sheet and name it "Drill down".

2. Place **Order Date** on the **Columns** and **Sales** on the **Rows**. Tableau automatically creates a hierarchy starting with Year. The + sign in front of the field indicates that it has a hierarchy and can be drilled down.

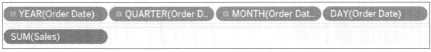

3. To drill down to the lower levels, click on the **+** symbol

4. Any level of Hierarchy can be removed by simply dragging it out of the view canvas or right click on the pill and select **Remove**.

Exercise

How Analytics pane works

1. Use the same workbook, Chapter2-VisualizationBasics.
2. Create a new sheet, by clicking on the new sheet button at the bottom of your Tableau desktop screen
3. Place **Order Date** on the **Columns** and **Sales** on **Rows**. Create a bar chart using **Show Me**.
4. Click on **Analytics** tab next to the Data pane. Drag **Constant Line** on the view.

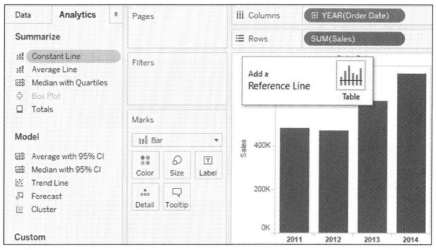

5. It will plot a **Reference line** on the bars with a constant value displayed. This value can be changed in the edit box or right- click on the reference line to see more details.

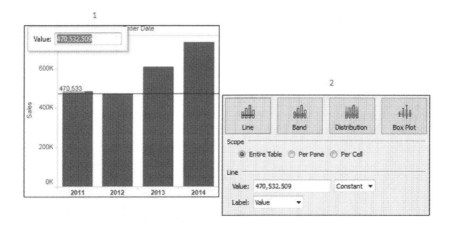

3
Data Transformation

Data Transformation involves transforming the structure of the data to meet the business need. Some examples of transformation may involve, renaming fields, aggregating data, changing the datatype, combining or splitting fields.
In this chapter, you will learn different ways in which data and data connection can be transformed and prepared for the ease of development and usage.

❖ Open Chapter2-ConnectingtoData and save it as Chap3-DataTransformation and follow along. You can save the files as twb or twbx.

Data Transformation Basics

1. Data sources in Tableau can be **Renamed**. Edit data source to add more tables or modify joins. Make changes to the datasource by clicking on the Datasource tab on the **bottom left** or right clicking on the datasource name on top and selecting **Edit Data Source**.
2. Right clicking on the datasource, provides different options

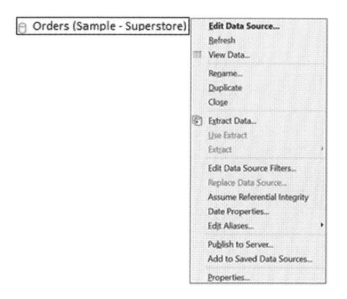

3. Datasource can be renamed, copied or published on the server. User can change from **Live** connection to **Extract data** and **Refresh** extracts. Date properties can be set and filters can be added.

4. Data type of a Field can be changed in the Data window by clicking on **ABC** next to the field.

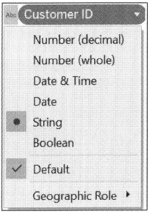

5. Pull down menu on the right of the field provide more options

6. The following options are available
   a. **Add to Sheet**, adds field to the view canvas.
   b. **Show Filter** is used to make a field act like a Quick filter.
   c. **Duplicate** a field to create a copy of the field.
   d. **Rename** a field to give a Business friendly name.
   e. **Hide** unused fields.
   f. **Aliases** can be created to provide alternate names to the value of the field. E.g. Region South can be aliased to SZ.
   g. **Create,** this option is used to create a calculated field, Group, Set or parameter.
   h. **Transform** option splits a composite field into different fields.

a. **Convert to Measure**. A dimension field can be converted to a Measure or vice versa.
b. **Change data type**, is used to change the data type of the field.
c. **Geographic role,** you can assign any field to a geographic role or change the property of the location based field.
d. **Default properties,** is used to provide default property to a field such as comment, color, shape or sort.
e. **Group by**. Related fields can be grouped in folders.
f. **Folder,** this option helps in creating folders to group related data elements. It works in conjunction with Group By.
g. **Hierarchy** of data elements can be created such as Country/State/City or Category/Subcategory.
h. **Replace References**. During data refresh underlying data changes, reference to a field can be replaced.
i. **Describe**. This option will give more information about the field. This is helpful in gaining details about a renamed field.

7. Fields prefixed by = are calculated fields.
8. In the data section, Fields like **Measure Names** under **Dimensions** and **Number of Records** and **Measure Values** under **Measures** are automatically generated by Tableau.
9. Changes to the datasource fields can also be made by clicking on the **Data Source** tab on the bottom left, navigate to Data connections window and select **Manage Metadata option**.

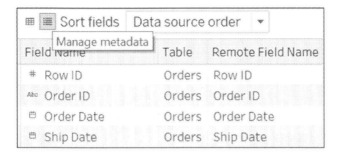

Transforming data in Sample-Superstore data source

In this section, we will apply data transformation to the data source.

Download Sample workbook - http://tabsoft.co/2pQO4WE
Exercise
Use the recently saved Chap3- DataTransformation to perform the following transformations.

1. Right click on the **Postal code** and click **Rename**

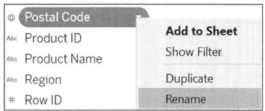

   Rename Postal Code to ZipCode.
2. Create hierarchy using the location related fields such as Country, State, City, ZipCode
   In the data section, ctrl + click and select **City**, **Country**, **State** and **ZipCode** fields. Right click and select **Hierarchy**. Name this hierarchy as **Location**.

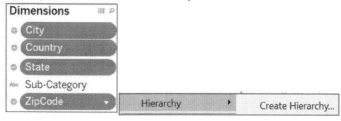

Drag and drop the fields to give the correct order

❖ **Optional Exercise:**
Create hierarchy using the fields **Product ID, Product Name, Category** and **Sub-Category** and name it **Products**.

3. Create a **folder** to organize dimension fields. Right click on **Customer ID** field and select **Group By – Folder.** Click on **Folder** and select **Create Folder**

Create a Folder **Customer** to organize Customer related fields.

4. Navigate to the field **Region**, right click and select **Aliases.** Change **Value (Alias)** of values as follows

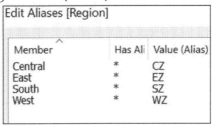

5. In the data section, navigate to the **Measures,** right click on **Sales** and select **Default Properties – Number format.** Select the option **Currency (Custom)** and click OK.

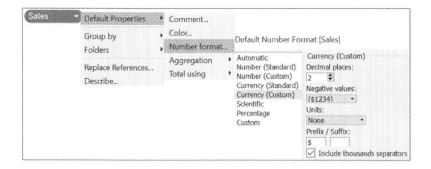

6. Save the datasource, by right clicking on the data source name on the top and selecting **Add to Saved Data Sources**. It will save as **.tds** file.
   Save it under
   \My Tableau Repository\Datasources\10.1\en_US-US. This saves all the information about the datasource. Name it Superstore_Training.tds.

   Other developers and power users can use this datasource file to create visualizations.

7. Datasource can also be published to the server, by right clicking on the data source name and selecting **Publish to Server**. Other developers and power users can download this datasource file from the server to create visualizations.
   To publish datasource to the server, access to Tableau Server is required.

8. DataSource can be extracted to a **.tde** file. To create an extract, right click on the datasource name and select **Extract data**.

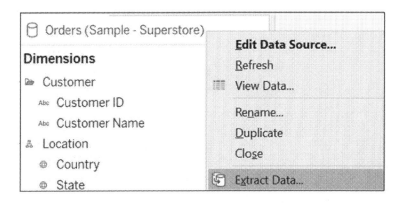

Look for .tde or **Tableau Extract** file in your data source folder.

When data is extracted and tde file is created, the symbol of the datasource changes in the data window.

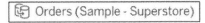

9. Save Chapter3- DataTransformation.twb.
10. Make a copy of this twb and rename it as **OnlyData.twb**. This workbook can be used in other exercises in the coming sections.

❖ TDE file is a snapshot of the data. It also provides the option to get a subset of the data by using filters.

Optional Exercise:

1. Explore and change the default properties of other measure fields.

2. Create a sheet using the **Region** field and **Sales** field. See how the values in Region field displays.

Loading Crosstab table/Sales Report

Consider this example;
You have received **SalesReport_10.xls** from the Sales
Department of your company. Your task is to load this report
and drive meaningful results.

On your machine, navigate to
\My Tableau Repository\Datasources\10.1\en_US-US
Double click on Sales report_10.xls and check the file.

This report contains - **Report name** and **Date**. It also contains
Employee Info such as, Employee ID, Category and Sales done
by an Employee in different Years.
If this report is loaded in Tableau without any transformation,
it will be difficult to drive useful information.
For example,
Performing aggregation will be difficult. It will also be difficult
to get Year by Year trend.
To get the correct results in the visualization, the table should
be transformed to structure like the **ExpectedTable** format.
Refer to "ExpectedTable" sheet in the SalesReport_10.xls.

Download Sample workbook - http://tabsoft.co/2pQZgm6
Exercise

Use Chap3-DataTransformation and save as Chap3-Crosstab.
To load this sheet in the correct format, follow the steps
mentioned below:

1. From main-menu select **Data – New Data Source**.

2. Browse to SalesReport_10.xls
3. Drag **SalesReport** to **Drag sheets here**
4. Review the file format in the preview window.

Abc	Abc	#	#	#	#
SalesReport	SalesReport	SalesReport	SalesReport	SalesReport	SalesReport
F1	**F2**	**F3**	**F4**	**F5**	**F6**
Sales Report	May 1st 2015	*null*	*null*	*null*	*null*
Employee ID	Sub-Category	2,011.00	2,012.00	2,013.00	2,014.00
CZ-001	Accessories	25,014.27	40,523.96	41,895.85	59,946.23
CZ-002	Appliances	15,313.63	23,241.29	26,050.32	42,926.93

The format of the data does not look good - Headers are not correct. There are Nulls on the first row. Tableau recognizes this and suggests to use Data Interpreter. This option will appear on the left, just below the connections.

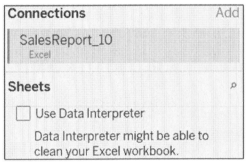

5. Check **Use Data Interpreter** option. The nulls in column headers have gone and the preview shows the correct column Headers now.

Abc	Abc	#	#	#	#
SalesReport	SalesReport	SalesReport	SalesReport	SalesReport	SalesReport
Employee ID	**Sub-Categ...**	**2013**	**2014**	**2015**	**2016**
CZ-001	Accessories	25,014.27	40,523.96	41,895.85	59,946.23
CZ-002	Appliances	15,313.63	23,241.29	26,050.32	42,926.93
EZ-003	Art	6,057.98	6,236.83	5,909.65	8,914.32
EZ-004	Binders	43,488.27	37,453.10	49,485.18	72,986.19

Click on **Review results** to get more info on how Data Interpreter worked on your data.

6. The Data Interpreter option is not displayed, if data is already in Tableau readable form. This option is also not available if
   a. Excel data has more than 2000 columns.
   b. Excel data contains more than 3000 rows and more than 150 columns.

   According to the "ExpectedTable" sheet, Years should be displayed in one column. To achieve this, click on 2013 and Shift+click on 2016. From the drop-down on the far right select **Pivot**

#	#	#	#	▼	
SalesReport	SalesReport	SalesReport	SalesReport	Rename	
2013	2014	2015	2016	Copy Values	
25,014.27	40,523.96	41,895.85	59,946.2	Hide	
15,313.63	23,241.29	26,050.32	42,926.9	Create Calculated Field...	
6,057.98	6,236.83	5,909.65	8,914.3	Pivot	

7. Pivot option will combine info from columns and rows into two new columns – Pivot field names and Pivot field values

Abc	#	Abc	Abc
Pivot	Pivot	SalesReport	SalesReport
Pivot Field ...	Pivot Field ...	Employee ID	Sub-Categ...
2013	25,014.27	CZ-001	Accessories
2013	15,313.63	CZ-002	Appliances
2013	6,057.98	EZ-003	Art
2013	43,488.27	EZ-004	Binders
2013	20,036.68	EZ-005	Bookcases

Rename **Pivot field names** to **Year**. Rename **Pivot field values** to **Sales**.

To rename, either double click on the field header or click on the second drop down next to "Abc".

8. As you know the **Employee ID** field is a combination of Region and Employee ID, we can **split** this field into two

9. fields. We can split this column into 2 columns using "–" as a delimiter.

10. To perform this, click on the second drop-down menu next to "Abc" on **Employee ID** and select Split.

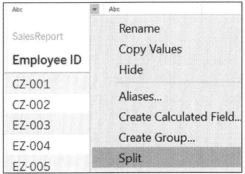

Now we have two new fields, suffixed with Split 1 and Split 2

11. We can rename these fields to reflect the business names. Rename the first Emp ID – Split1 field as **Emp-Region** and second one as **Emp-Number**.

Year	Sales	Employee ID	Sub-Categ...	Emp-Region	Emp-Number
2013	25,014....	CZ-001	Accessories	CZ	1
2013	15,313....	CZ-002	Appliances	CZ	2
2013	6,057.98	EZ-003	Art	EZ	3
2013	43,488....	EZ-004	Binders	EZ	4
2013	20,036....	EZ-005	Bookcases	EZ	5

Save Chapter3-CrossTab.twb file.

Data Blending

❖ Save Chapter3-CrossTab as Chapter3-DataBlending.

After completing the previous exercise, the twb file contains two data sources - Orders (Sample - Superstore) and SalesReport (SalesReport_10).
For analysis, it is required to create visualization using these two data sources.
If a visualization is created using fields from both the data sources, a warning will be generated.
To recreate this, drag **State** from data source Orders (Sample - Superstore) on the **Columns** and **Sales** from SalesReport (SalesReport_10) on to **Rows**.

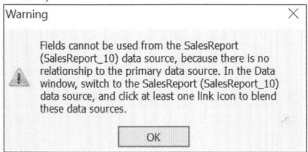

Data blending can help in such scenarios.
Data blending is a process that combines data from multiple data sources.
Data blending Basics:
> • At least one common dimension field should exist between the two data sources.
> • Data blending can be performed by making the columns common by renaming them.
> Alternatively, if a common dimension does not exist, then edit the relationship between the datasources.
> To edit the relationship, go to menu and select **Data/Edit Relationships**.

• These common columns behave similar to joins between the tables, except that instead of sending the query to one datasource, data blending executes separately and joins the aggregated results.

• The **blue check** on the datasource indicates the primary datasource.

The datasource, from which a field is first placed on the view is considered as the primary datasource. These data sources can be switched to change the direction of the blending.

• By default, data blending is similar to left outer join. By changing the primary and secondary data sources and filtering nulls, the join can be changed.

• Field/data from primary datasource is used to fetch the records from each of the datasources.

• Data blending is used when the datasource and data connections are different.

• Data blending works per sheet and it is not applied globally to all the sheets in the workbook.

Download Sample workbook - http://tabsoft.co/2oZHbgP
Exercise

Apply data blending to get the data from both the data sources.

1. In Chapter3-DataBlending.twb, the two data sources contain a common field **Sub-Category**.
2. Create a new sheet and name it **Data blending**.
3. Drag **Sub-category** from Orders (Sample - Superstore) and **Sales** from SalesReport (SalesReport_10).

Notice the data sources. Sample-Superstore has a **blue** checkmark and   SalesReport has an orange check mark.

The Blue checkmark indicates the primary datasource and an **Orange** checkmark indicates the secondary datasource.

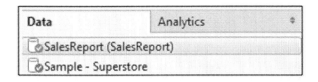

In SalesReport.xls datasource, notice an Orange link symbol next to Sub-category.

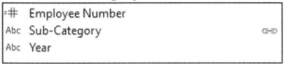

This shows that two data sources are blended on the Sub- Category field. If not, then click on the grey link ⊏⌿⊃

4. From the previous exercise, we know that **Region** in Sample-Superstore is the same as **Emp-Region** in SalesReport.

Therefore these two fields can also be used for blending. Since the names of the fields are different, navigate to menu- Data/Edit Relationships and create **custom relationship**.

Joins in Tableau

Joins are used to combine the results of two or more tables. Joins occur on Primary key and foreign keys between two tables or between matching columns.

Joins in Tableau are similar to SQL joins – Inner Join, Left join, right join and outer join.

> • **Inner join**. Returns the matching rows between the tables
> • **Left join**. Returns all the rows from the left table and the matching rows from the right table.
> • **Right join**. Returns all the rows from the right table and the matching rows from the left table.
> • **Full Outer**. Returns rows from both the tables. It is a combination of Left and Right joins.

> ❖ Depending on your datasource, Tableau may not show you the option to use all types of joins.
> Tableau always suggests join columns which can be modified.

Connecting to Access db/Understanding Joins

To understand joins, we will use the Access database **Emp_Dept_10.mdb**.

Explore the database. It contains 3 tables for Emp, Dept and Salary.

Emp has 7 rows of data.

Dept has 6 rows of data.

Salary has 4 rows of data.

Download Sample workbook - http://tabsoft.co/2ppF89i

Exercise

> 1. Launch Tableau desktop. In the **Connect** window, click on **Access** to connect.
> 2. Browse to Emp_Dept_10.mdb on your machine under **My Tableau Repository/DataSources**.

You will follow the same steps to connect to any other relational database.

3. Drag **Emp** table to "Drag Tables here" and see the count of rows. It shows 7 rows.
4. Now drag **Dept** table. Tableau automatically inner joins the tables based on the matching field DepartmentID. If you think this is incorrect, you can always modify the join condition. Inner join displays the matching rows between the tables.

5. In this case, the number of rows will be 4

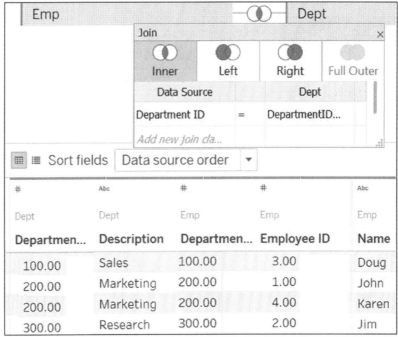

Dept Departmen...	Dept Description	Emp Departmen...	Emp Employee ID	Emp Name
100.00	Sales	100.00	3.00	Doug
200.00	Marketing	200.00	1.00	John
200.00	Marketing	200.00	4.00	Karen
300.00	Research	300.00	2.00	Jim

6. From the join box, change join to **Left** and see the results.

Left join takes all the rows from the first table (Emp) and matching rows from the second table (Dept). If the matching rows in the second table do not exist, they will be displayed as null. In these tables, Emp has Dept 901,501 and 601 which do not exist in the Dept table. The corresponding values in Dept table do not exist and are therefore displayed as Null. The Number of rows is this case is 7.

DepartmentID ... ⋥	Description	Department ID	Employee ID	Name
300.00	Research	300.00	2.00	Jim
200.00	Marketing	200.00	1.00	John
200.00	Marketing	200.00	4.00	Karen
100.00	Sales	100.00	3.00	Doug
null	null	901.00	5.00	Kim
null	null	501.00	7.00	Sam
null	null	601.00	8.00	Raj

7. From the join box, change join to **Right** and see the results.
Right join will display all the rows from the Right/Dept table and all matching rows from the left table/Emp.
The number of rows in this is also 7 because there are 2 employees working in Department ID 200

DepartmentID ... ᵼ	Description	Department ID	Employee ID	Name
800.00	Security	null	null	null
700.00	IT	null	null	null
400.00	Training	null	null	null
300.00	Research	300.00	2.00	Jim
200.00	Marketing	200.00	1.00	John
200.00	Marketing	200.00	4.00	Karen
100.00	Sales	100.00	3.00	Doug

8. Notice that the Full Outer join option is greyed out. That is the restriction from the datasource. Access database does not support full outer join. You can simulate full outer join by writing a query using **Custom SQL.**

9. Save your file as **Chap3-Joins**.

Writing Custom SQL

Custom SQL option is useful in writing complex queries or when you have to copy/paste an existing database query.
Exercise
To perform Full Outer join, we will use the Custom SQL option.

1. Remove all the tables you have so far on the screen. To remove ,click on the Table, use the pull down menu symbol on the right of the table and select **Remove**.

2. To define Custom SQL, drag **New Custom SQL** to "Drag Tables here" canvas

In the Edit Custom SQL box, type your SQL

Edit Custom SQL

```
Select * from Emp
Left join Dept on Emp.DepartmentID = Dept.DepartmentID

Union

Select * from Emp
Right join Dept on Emp.DepartmentID = Dept.DepartmentID
```

You can create your desired visualization using these joined datasets.

Adding Another Data source

In Tableau 10, you can also connect and join to another datasource. This datasource can be a different database or an Excel or a csv file. These types of joins are also referred as Cross-table joins.

In the next exercise, we will add another datasource **Shipper_Info_10.csv**. This file contains the Shipper info for the Orders table in Sample-Superstore.xls.

Download Sample workbook - http://tabsoft.co/2pBO7ot
Exercise
1. Launch Tableau desktop. Create a new workbook.

2. To create new data source, connect to Sample-Superstore.xls. Drag **Orders** table to **Drag Sheet here** section

3. Click on **Add** in the **Connections** window

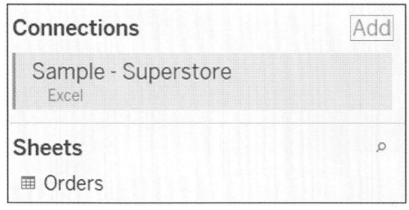

4. Browse to file Shipper_Info_10.csv which is located in My Tableau Repository/DataSources folder

5. Tableau will create an automatic join based on the common field. You can always modify this join.

6. Save this file as Chap3-AddingAnotherDataSource

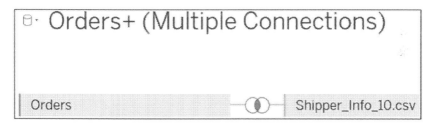

These types of join provide huge advantage as compared to Data blending. Data blending is always left-outer join and can have performance problems. Cross-table join can be of any kind.

4
Calculations in Tableau

Calculations are created to enhance the dashboard. Tableau takes granular or detail level data and aggregates them in the view. Calculations help in extending the usage of aggregations. Calculations also help in creating dimensions or measures which do not exist in the datasource.

Before going further into calculations, let's understand a few important concepts:
- Aggregating Data
- Granularity of Data.

Aggregating Data

When a field from Measures is placed on a shelf, Tableau automatically aggregates the data. Default is **Sum**. You can change the default aggregation to other types, by clicking on the pill, navigating to Measure (Sum) and selecting other aggregation types.

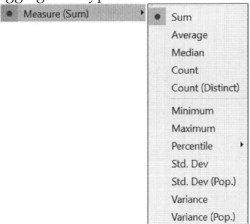

❖ Tableau automatically aggregates a measure, but you can disaggregate a data by navigating to the **Menu/Analysis** and deselecting **Aggregate Measures**.

Dimensions can also be aggregated. The options available for dimensions are Minimum, Maximum, Count, Count (Distinct)

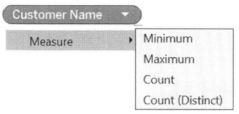

Attr is also an aggregation function that is applied to the dimensions.

Attr (Expression) returns value only if it has one value for all the rows, otherwise it returns *.

Download Sample workbook - http://tabsoft.co/2qmpTiE
Exercise
Understanding Attr
Consider the following example to understand Attr.
1. Open OnlyData.twb. This workbook just contains data and will be used in different exercises.
2. Save it as Chap4-Aggregation.
3. Create a new sheet and name it **Profit by RegionCity**.
4. Place **Region** and **City** on **Rows** and **Profit** on **Text** under Marks. This will create a table.
5. In **Dimensions**, right click on **Region** dimension and select **Show Filter**
6. Right click on **City** dimension and select **Show Filter** and create a table like the following.

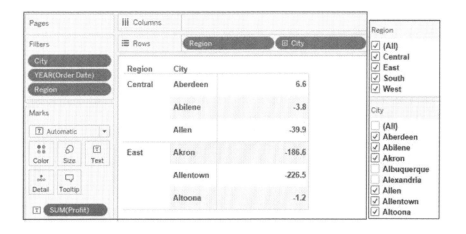

7. Notice that Region - Central and East have multiple Cities.
   Now due to some business requirement, you need to create a calculation when **Region** Central is selected.
8. Create a **calculated field** by navigating to **Menu/_A_nalysis – _C_reate Calculated field** and name it **Profit By Region / City**. Use the following expression

   If [Region]= "Central" then Sum([Profit])
   END

   The expression will show error

9. This error has occurred because there are multiple rows for Region = Central in the data source. You need to aggregate Region to get one row.
   Modify your expression as
   If ATTR([Region])= "Central" then Sum([Profit])
   END

10. Test your expression, by duplicating the previous sheet and using Profit by Region/City in place of Profit.

A Word about Agg

By default, Tableau aggregates a measure placed on the view canvas like Sum (Sales) or Sum (Profit). When an aggregated measure is used in a calculation and this calculation is placed on the view canvas, it shows **Agg** in front of the calculated column.

It means that aggregation is built within the calculation. This aggregation cannot be changed.

You can see this in the previous exercise – there is AGG in front of Profit by Region/City.

Granularity of Data

Data granularity refers to the level of detail or depth of data in a table or view.

For e.g. Data can be stored at a Year or Month level. If data is stored at the Year level then it is at the lower granularity.

If the data is stored at the Month level, then it is at a higher granularity.

Data at Year level will have less number of rows than data at the Month level.

Example

Year level of data – one row for 2016

Year	Sales
2016	12000

Month level of data – 12 rows of data.

Year	Month	Sales
2016	Jan	1000
2016	Feb	1000
2016	Mar	1000
2016	Apr	1000
2016	May	1000
2016	Jun	1000
2016	Jul	1000
2016	Aug	1000
2016	Sep	1000
2016	Oct	1000
2016	Nov	1000
2016	Dec	1000
	Total	12000

Total in both the cases will still be the same.

In Tableau, granularity of data is defined by the **Dimension** fields.

The **Dimension** field dropped on **Detail** will change the granularity of the visualization.

Dropping a **measure** on the Detail will have no effect.

❖ Open OnlyData.twb and save as Chapter4-Granularity

Download Sample workbook - http://tabsoft.co/2qxZ1sJ
Exercise

1. Double click on **Profit** and **Sales**, Tableau will display just one Mark which is for Sum (Sales) and Sum (Profit).This is the sum in the entire source data.

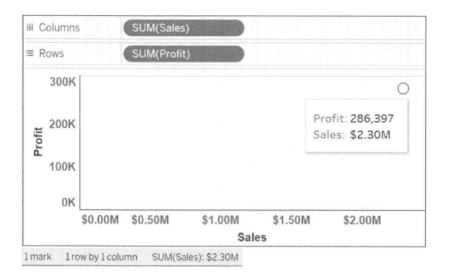

Profit: 286,397
Sales: $2.30M

1 mark   1 row by 1 column   SUM(Sales): $2.30M

If you want to calculate these values for a specific level of detail or granularity, you will do so by adding **Dimensions** to the view.

2. Place **Category** on the **Color**. Tableau will display 3 **Marks**. It displays Sum (Sales) and Sum (Profit) for each of the Category.

3. Now add **Region** to **Size** and you will see **12 Marks**. Now Tableau displays Sum (Sales) and Sum (Profit) for each category in different regions.

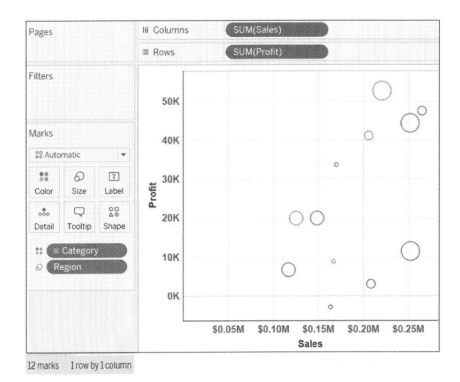

Changing the Region to another shelf such as **Shape** will not change the granularity of the view; you will still see 12 marks.

Detail is a way of affecting the granularity of the data without dropping in fields into shape, size or color.

3. Now drop **Product Name** to the **Detail** shelf. Product Name does not have a separate shape or color but aggregation in the view has changed. Marks reflect the changed combination.

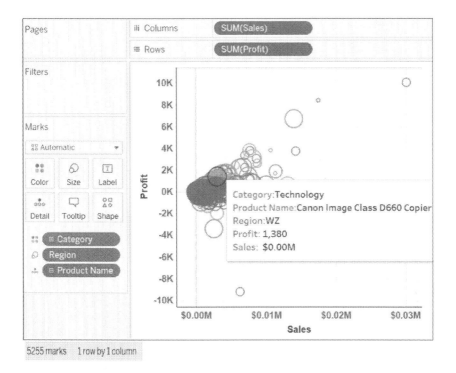

Category:Technology
Product Name:Canon Image Class D660 Copier
Region:WZ
Profit: 1,380
Sales: $0.00M

5255 marks   1 row by 1 column

Calculated fields

❖ Open Chapter3-DataTransformation.twb and
   save as Chapter4-Calculations.twb

Calculated field Basics

• Calculated fields can be created for dimensions and
measures.

• Calculated fields are created by defining a formula. It
uses functions provided by Tableau.

• Calculated field is created by right clicking anywhere
on the data window and selecting **Create Calculated
Field.**

```
        Create Calculated Field...
```

Calculated field can also be created from
Menu/Analysis – Create Calculated Field.

Calculated fields can also be created directly on the view canvas – Columns or Rows shelfs.

• Calculated field can use any of the Tableau defined functions such as

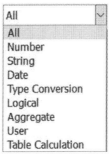

• In the data window = sign in front of a field indicates that the field is a calculated field.

• Any Text in the calculation should be enclosed in " ".

• Tableau provides different ways of creating calculated field, such as, regular calculations, Table calculations, Quick Table calculations, Level of Detail calculations (LOD)

Types of Calculations

1. **Regular Calculation**. This calculation is sent to the data source for processing and the result is returned to Tableau.

2. **Table Calculation**. Calculation occurs on top of the "returned result set". Calculation processing happens in Tableau.

A Table Calculation is written like any other calculation and uses the Table Calculation functions. It can also be built by using the set of predefined calculations called **Quick Table Calculation**.

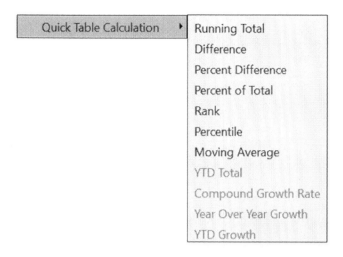

3. **Level of Detail (LOD) calculation**. This calculation computes aggregation that is out of the level of detail of the view.

Download Sample workbook - http://tabsoft.co/2pz6b0r
Exercise - Creating Regular Calculation

1. Use previously saved Chapter4-Calculations.twb. Create a new sheet and call it **Regular Calculation**.
2. From **Measures**, select **Sales**, right click and select **Create -> Calculated Field.**
3. Name and define your calculation as below

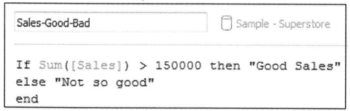

Calculated field also displays the name of the data source on which this calculation is created.
4. Place **Sales** to the **Columns** shelf and **Category** to the **Rows** shelf. Click on + next to Category and drill-down to Sub-Category. Drop newly created Calculation "Sales-Good-Bad" to the **Color** card.

Your dashboard will look like the one below

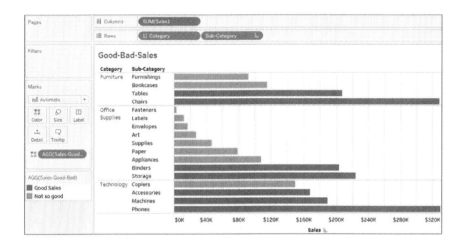

Table Calculation

Table calculation helps in answering business questions.

Question. What is the running sum of profit?

> 1. Use previously saved Chapter4-Calculations.twb.
> 2. Create a new sheet and name it **Table Calculation**.
> 3. Right click on the **Profit** in the data window and select **Create Calculated Field.**
> 4. Use Table Calculation in the Calculation editor and use **Running Sum**. Since we are finding "Running sum of (sum of) Profit", specify Sum with Profit.

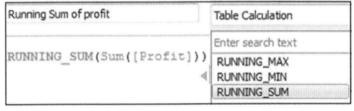

> 5. Create a visualization with this Table Calculation. Place **Order Date** on the **Rows** Shelf and drill down to Year/Quarter. Double click on **Profit** and place calculated field **Running sum of Profit** on the Table.

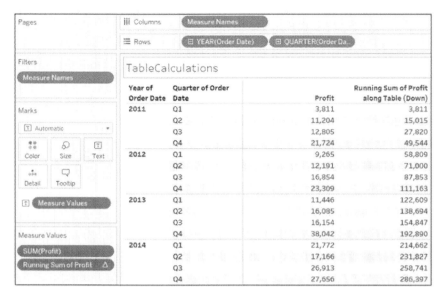

△ Delta symbol on "Running sum of profit" pill indicates that it is a Table Calculation.

This calculation is done on top of the calculation Sum (Profit). Since Table Calculation occurs on the result set, changing fields in the view, changes the result.

Modifying Table Calculations

Once Table Calculation has been created, it can be modified to answer different questions.

From "Running Sum of Profit" pull down menu, check options under **Compute using**.

1. Duplicate the "Table Calculation" Sheet and name it **Modify Table calculations**.

2. Click on the Running Sum of Profit **pull down menu** and make the above selection in the **Compute using** for **Order Date**.

3. Use pull down menu again and this time, select **Edit Table Calculations**.

Compute using, will give you different options on how Table calculations should be done. Select different methods and see how the chart changes.

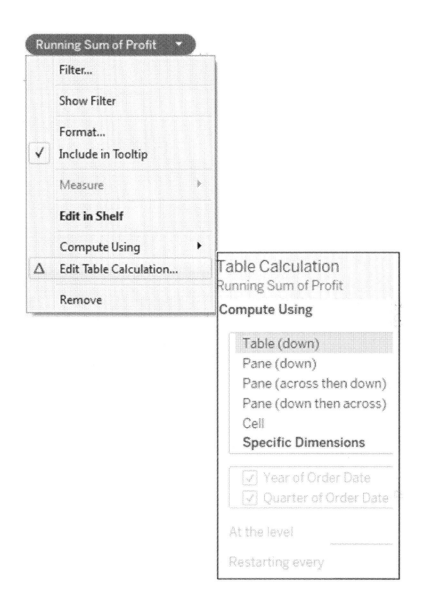

Quick Table Calculations

Table calculations can be defined like any other calculations or using predefined Table Calculations called **Quick Table calculations**. The following types of Quick table calculations are available.

Quick Table Calculation ▸	Running Total
	Difference
	Percent Difference
	Percent of Total
	Rank
	Percentile
	Moving Average
	YTD Total
	Compound Growth Rate
	Year Over Year Growth
	YTD Growth

The above visualization can also be created using the Quick Table calculations.

1. Use Chapter4-Calculations, create a new Sheet and call it QuickTableCalculation.

2. Place **Order Date** on the **Rows** Shelf and drill down to Year/Quarter.

3. Place **Profit** on the Label under Marks. Tableau will automatically use Sum aggregate function and create a Table.

4. Click on the Sum(Profit) pill and select **Quick Table Calculation/Running Total**.

5. You will get the same results as when we used the Table Calculation above for "Running Sum of Profit.

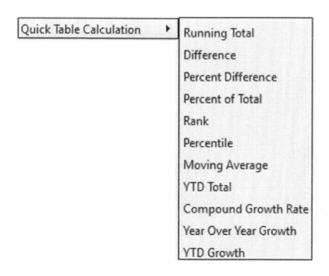

Rank Table Calculation

To calculate the Rank of a measure, Table Calculation can be used.

Exercise

Find the Rank of each State by Sales?

    1. Use Chapter4-Calculations and create a new sheet **Rank**.

    2. Right click on **Sales** and select **Create/Calculated field Rank of Sum(Sales)**

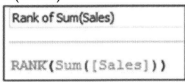

    3. Place **State** to **Rows** and **Rank of Sales** to columns

    4. Click on [T] on the tool bar and sort the chart in ascending. You can see the States ranked by Sum (Sales). Since there are so many states, it will be difficult to get all the States on the visualization.

    5. Put a filter for **States** and select few states.

Drop **Sales** on the ToolTip so that when you hover over the individual bars, it will display rank with the Sales.

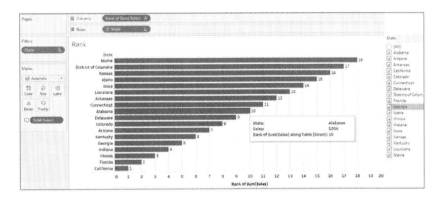

Level of Detail Calculation (LOD)

❖ Open OnlyData.twb and save it as Chapter4-LOD.twb.

LOD calculation computes aggregation that is outside the "level of detail" of the view.

❖ Remember that dimension in **Detail** controls the aggregation of the visualization in the view.

Syntax:

{Include [Region],[Segment],[Order Priority]: Sum(Sales)}

LOD Basics

• LOD expressions are included in curly braces.

• The first word inside curly braces is a **Keyword**. This keyword can be **Fixed, Include** or **Exclude**. **Keywords** define the scope of expression execution. Expression can be specified without a keyword too. In that case, the scope is the entire Table.

After the keyword, "**dimension/s**" is specified on which the keyword will act on. Multiple dimensions can be used. These dimensions should be separated by comma and should be from the same data source. Combined fields cannot be used.

• : completes the level of detail and the **aggregation** is specified after that.

Aggregation cannot be **Attr** or a **Table calculation**.

Download Sample workbook - http://tabsoft.co/2qxZ1sJ
Exercise

To understand LOD concept, let us review an example

1. Use Chapter4-LOD.
   Let us calculate the Average (profit) for all the **Orders** by each **City**.

2. Create a visualization
    a. by placing **City** and then **Profit** on the view canvas.

    From the pull-down menu of Profit, change aggregation of Profit to **Avg**.

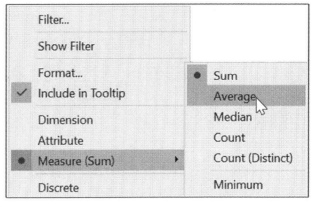

Since City is a geographical location, Tableau will automatically create a Map.

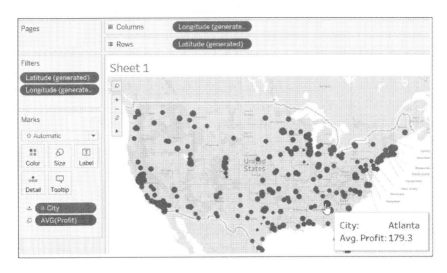

3. Since there are so many cities, we can put a filter on **State** and **City**.

In the Dimensions window, right click on **State** and select **Show Filter**. Do the same for City.

Filter State to Georgia, you will see only GA cities. From **Show Me**, change the chart type to Bar.

Since we are just interested in **City**, drag out County and State one by one out of the view canvas.

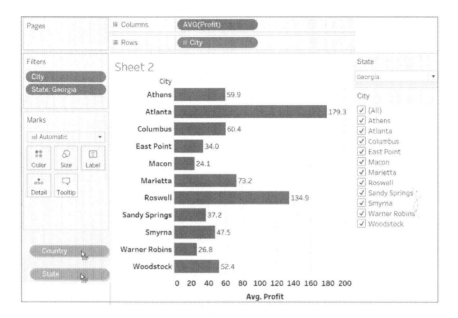

4. Check to see if this is the right average. Right click on the chart and select **View data** and on the view data sheet, select **Full Data**. You will see that there are many Orders with duplicate Order ID's . One such OrderId is highlighted in the picture below.

These are the multiple line items on a single item.

Category	City	Country	Customer ID	Customer Name	Order Date	Order ID	Product ID	Pi
Office Supplies	Athens	United States	JO-15145	Jack O'Briant	1/7/2011	CA-2011-106054	OFF-AR-10002399	Di
Technology	Roswell	United States	EH-13990	Erica Hackney	1/16/2011	CA-2011-103366	TEC-AC-10003628	Lc
Office Supplies	Athens	United States	RD-19585	Rob Dowd	4/2/2011	CA-2011-164315	OFF-AP-10003842	Ei
Office Supplies	Athens	United States	RD-19585	Rob Dowd	4/2/2011	CA-2011-164315	OFF-PA-10004248	Xe
Technology	Athens	United States	RD-19585	Rob Dowd	4/2/2011	CA-2011-164315	TEC-PH-10001128	Mi
Office Supplies	Marietta	United States	VM-21685	Valerie Mitchum	4/7/2011	CA-2011-165806	OFF-PA-10003441	Xe
Technology	Marietta	United States	VM-21685	Valerie Mitchum	4/7/2011	CA-2011-165806	TEC-PH-10004922	Ri
Office Supplies	Roswell	United States	SV-20785	Stewart Visinsky	6/2/2011	CA-2011-100895	OFF-AR-10004511	Se
Office Supplies	Roswell	United States	SV-20785	Stewart Visinsky	6/2/2011	CA-2011-100895	OFF-ST-10001490	Hi
Technology	Roswell	United States	SV-20785	Stewart Visinsky	6/2/2011	CA-2011-100895	TEC-PH-10001425	Mi
Furniture	Atlanta	United States	SG-20470	Sheri Gordon	7/26/2011	CA-2011-116190	FUR-CH-10000553	Mi
Furniture	Atlanta	United States	SG-20470	Sheri Gordon	7/26/2011	CA-2011-116190	FUR-FU-10000719	Di
Office Supplies	Atlanta	United States	SG-20470	Sheri Gordon	7/26/2011	CA-2011-116190	OFF-LA-10002762	Ai
Office Supplies	Woodstock	United States	LL-16840	Lauren Leatherbury	8/12/2011	CA-2011-153927	OFF-BI-10000138	Ai

So, the Average shown by Tableau is the **Average (Profit) of every Line item in the city**.

Our objective is to find the Average (Profit) by Orders not by the line Item.

Even if there are multiple Line items in one Order, we have to compute at the Order Level.

Level of Detail(LOD) expressions will be useful in such situations.

To calculate the Average (Profit) by Order ID, we need to follow two steps

- Calculate Sum (Profit) by Order ID
- Find the average of those values.

To calculate Sum (Profit) by Order ID, use LOD expression. Create a calculated field and call it – **Profit by Order ID**. Use the following expression

{Include [Order ID]: Sum(Profit)}

This will rollup/group all Line Items by their Order ID.

5. On the previous visualization, place "Profit by Order ID" on the view canvas and change the aggregation to **Average**.

6. See the comparison of the two averages. You will see big difference between the Averages because they are calculated at different granularity or level of detail. Left-side one is calculated for the every Line item and right- side one is calculated at the Order Level.

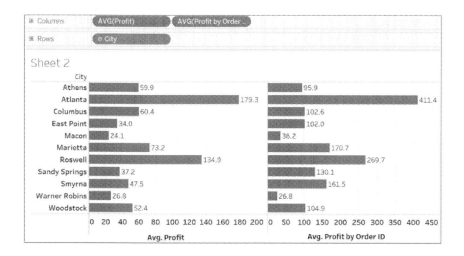

Even though Order ID is not in the view, we were able to calculate Average at that level using the LOD expression.

Understanding the LOD Expression

{Include [Order ID]: Sum(Profit)}

- **Include** calculates the values using the specified dimension. It also includes the dimension included in the view. In the above example, the **Include** expression specified Order ID in the expression and also used **City** dimension in the view.
- **Fixed** calculates the value using the specified dimension without using the dimensions in the view.
- **Exclude** will exclude the specified dimension even if it is used in the view.

Exercise – Fixed

1. Create a new sheet and name it LOD_Fixed.
2. Double click Zipcode and Profit. Tableau will create a Map. Change Sum (Profit) to Average (Profit). This will give you Average (Profit) for each zipcode.
3. Create a calculated field and name it **LOD_Fixed**. Use the following expression

   {Fixed [State]: SUM ([Profit])}

   This expression will compute at the **State** level. It will ignore the dimension in the view i.e. ZipCode.
4. Drop this "LOD_Fixed" on the **Detail** and change the aggregation to Average.
5. On the **Dimensions** window, right click on the **State** and select **Show Filter**. Select Georgia in the filter.
6. Hover over the circles on the Map. You will see a different value for **Avg(Profit)** but the same value for **Avg(LOD_Fixed).** Avg(Profit) is computed at the **Zipcode** level and Avg(LOD_Fixed) is calculated at the **State** level.

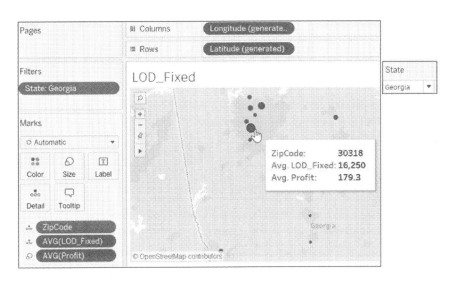

Exercise - Exclude

1. Create a new worksheet and name it LOD-Exclude.
2. Double click on City and Profit. You will get a Map with City and Sum (Profit) for each city.

Drag out Country and State out of the view canvas.
3. Create a **calculated field** and name it LOD-Exclude.
Use the following expression

$$\{EXCLUDE \ [City]: SUM([Profit])\}$$

Exclude will ignore the dimension **City** used in the view.
It will calculate the Sum (Profit) at the **Country** level.
Country is the highest level in the **Location** hierarchy.
4. Drop LOD-Exclude to **Detail**. Change aggregation to
Sum.
5. Now hover over the Map, you will find a different
Profit for each city but Sum (LOD_Exclude) is calculated
by ignoring the city dimension i.e. aggregated at the
Country level.

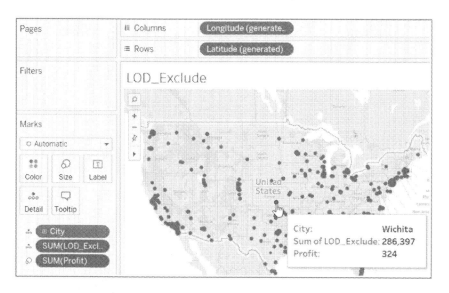

5
More Calculations

Apart from the calculation types we discussed in Chapter4, there are a few other types of calculations in Tableau. These calculations are

- Logical Calculation
- String Calculation
- Number Calculation
- Date calculation

Logical Calculation

Logical calculation determines if the condition is true or false. Logical functions in Tableau are

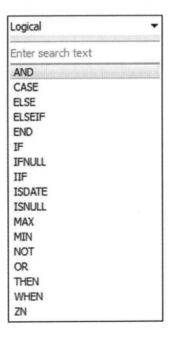

Exercise:
1. Open OnlyData.twb and save it as Chapter5-MoreCalculations.
2. Right click on **Profit** and create a calculated field **Profit for Region Central**
   Use the following expression.
   if ([Region]) = 'Central' then ([Profit])
   END
3. Create a new sheet and name it **Logical Calc**
4. Create a Table by using **Region** and **Profit for Region Central** calculated field.
5. You will get a table with values just in the Central Region.

String Calculation

String calculation performs string manipulation using Tableau's predefined String functions.

Some of the String functions available in Tableau are:

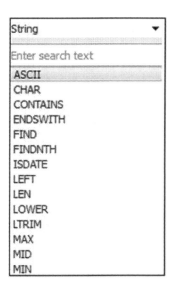

Exercise:

Question. Calculate Sum (Sales) for Product Name that contains "Deluxe" in the Name.

1. Create a new sheet – **String Calc**.
2. Click on **Product Name** and create a calculated field. Name it **Product Name- contains Deluxe** and use the following expression:

   Contains ([Product Name],"Deluxe")

3. Create a table using **Product Name** and **Sum(Sales)**
4. Place the calculated field **Product Name- contains Deluxe** on the filter and select "True".
5. You will get Product Names which contains "Deluxe".

The resulting chart will look like

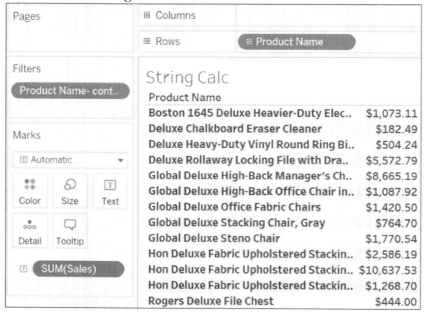

Number Calculation

Some of the Number function's available are:

Using Floor and Ceiling functions

Ceiling and Floor are very useful functions.

Ceiling rounds a number to the nearest integer of equal or greater value.

Floor rounds a number to the nearest integer of lesser or equal value.

Exercise

Question. Create a table with Sales, Floor(Sales) and Ceiling(Sales)

1. Use the same workbook, Chapter5-MoreCalculations. Create a new sheet and name it Floor_Ceiling
2. Make sure **Sales** - default property is set to 2 places of decimals.
3. Double click on **Category** and **Sales** to create a table.
4. Create two calculated fields, for using Floor and Ceiling functions

    Floor([Sales])

    CEILING([Sales])

Use this calculated fields in the table and see the results

Floor_Ceiling

Category	Sales	Ceiling	Floor
Furniture	$741,999.80	742,904	740,795
Office Supplies	$719,047.03	721,680	715,694
Technology	$836,154.03	836,589	834,815

Exercise

Question. A Table created in the **Logical Calc** sheet contains Null. How can we convert these null values into 0?

Use the previously calculated field "Profit for Region Central", right click and create a duplicate of this field and name it "Profit for Region Central_ZN"
Use the following expression.

ZN(if ([Region]) = 'Central' then ([Profit])
END)

Click on the sheet named **Logical Calc** , right click and **Duplicate** it. Name this sheet "ZN Function". Move the sheet to the last position.
Replace calc "Profit for Region Central" with "Profit for Region Central_ZN" and see that nulls are replaced by 0

ZN Function

Region	
CZ	39,706
EZ	0
SZ	0
WZ	0

Date Calculation

Date calculations are used to manipulate dates in Tableau. Date calculations use the Date Functions. Tableau provides a wide variety of date related functions.

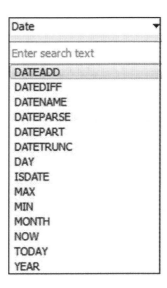

Exercise

Question How much time does it take for an Order to ship?

1. Create a new sheet and call it "Date calc".
2. Create a calculated column and name it "Time to Ship".

   To calculate the Time to ship, we will use the **DateDiff** function. This function returns the difference between two dates.

   Use the following expression

   DATEDIFF('day',[Order Date],[Ship Date])

3. On the view, create a table using Order ID and Date diff calculation to find the Time to ship.

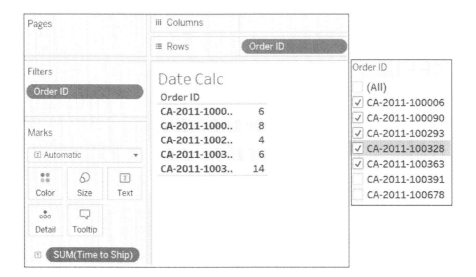

6
Filters and Parameters

A Filter restricts the data based on user defined conditions. It provides the context to the displayed data. Filters are similar to WHERE clause in SQL.
Filters can be applied in a variety of ways.

❖ Use OnlyData.twb and save as Chapter6-Filters

Filter Basics

• By default, all filters are applied independent of each other.

• Data source filters. These filters are applied during the data connection/extraction. These filters are applied to the entire dataset.

• Filters are created by using Dimension and Measure fields.

• Filters are created by placing a field on the **Filters** shelf.

Filters can be displayed as **Quick filters** by using **Show Filter** option.

• Filters can be applied to **All the sheets using the data source** or to a **specific worksheet**. Filters can be used to "Create Set". *Sets are discussed in a separate section.*

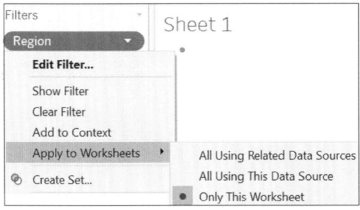

• **Context Filters** are created by placing a field on the filter shelf. Right click and select **Add to Context**.

It creates a subset of data. If a context filter is present, other filters are applied on this subset of data.

• Filters can also be applied on the visualization.

Select a data element, right click and choose the options

– **Keep only** or **Exclude**.

• Dimensions are discreet and Measures are continuous. When using a Measure field as a filter, you will get a range of values.

• Drag **Quantity** to the filter shelf and check out the options.

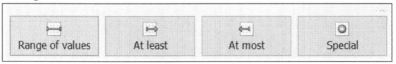

• A Filter can be applied while creating a data extract. Extract of the data can be created by right clicking on the datasource and selecting **Extract Data**.

Download Sample workbook - http://tabsoft.co/2qmH5Vh
Exercise – Data Source Filter

1. Use Chapter6-Filters workbook.
2. Right click on Sample-Superstore data source and select **Edit Data Source Filters**.
Data source filters can also be added at the time of creating new connections.
3. On the top right, you will see an option to add **Filter**. click on **Add**. In the **Edit Data Source Filters box** select **Add**. You will see a list of fields on which filters can be applied.
1. Select **Order Date** and select **Years**. Select 2013 and check **Exclude**. 2013 data will be restricted.

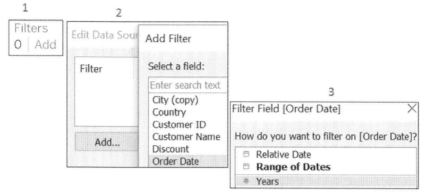

5. You can verify it by creating a filter on Order Date/Year in a sheet.

6. Click on the filter, get the pull down menu. Explore different options.

Exercise – Using Dimension and Measure as Filters

1. Use the previous Chapter6-Filters workbook.

2. On a new sheet, Double click on **Region**, **Segment** and **Sales**.

Place **Order Date** on the **Filters** Shelf. Select **Years**. You will see check boxes for the Years, click on **All** and Ok.

3. Right click on the **Year (Order Date)** filter and select **Show Filter**. The Filter will be displayed on the view canvas. You can use this filter to see the data for all the Years or specific Years.

4. Click on the **Years (Order Date)** filter on the right-hand-side, use the pull down menu and check out different options.

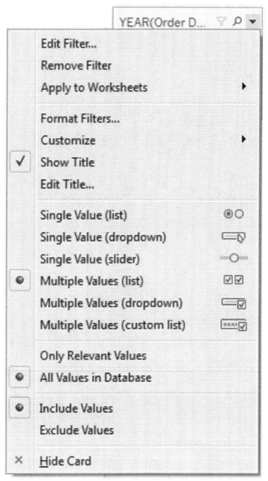

YEAR(Order D...

Edit Filter...	
Remove Filter	
Apply to Worksheets	▶
Format Filters...	
Customize	▶
✓ Show Title	
Edit Title...	
Single Value (list)	
Single Value (dropdown)	
Single Value (slider)	
Multiple Values (list)	
Multiple Values (dropdown)	
Multiple Values (custom list)	
Only Relevant Values	
All Values in Database	
Include Values	
Exclude Values	
× Hide Card	

5. On the view canvas, under **Region**, select Central or CZ and right click to see the options. Try **Keep only** or **Exclude** to see the difference.

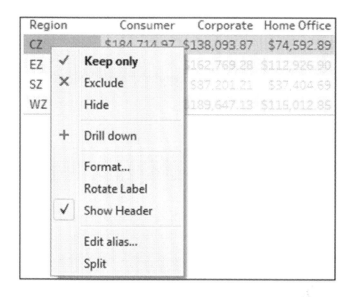

Region	Consumer	Corporate	Home Office
CZ	$184,714.97	$138,093.87	$74,592.89
EZ	✓ Keep only	162,769.28	$112,926.90
SZ	✗ Exclude	$87,201.21	$37,404.69
WZ	Hide	189,647.13	$115,012.85

+ Drill down

Format...

Rotate Label

✓ Show Header

Edit alias...

Split

6. To use Measure as a filter, on the data window, right click on **Sales** and select **Show Filter**. Since Sales is a measure, it will be displayed as a **Range of Values**. It will show as a slider on the view canvas. Use slider to see the change in the data.

7. To remove a filter, just drag it outside the view canvas or select Remove filter from the pull down menu.

Context Filters

By default all filters are applied independent of each other. In case of Context filter, a sub-set of data is created, something like a temp table. All the other filters act on this sub-set of data.

Exercise

1. Use the previous Chapter6-Filters workbook. Create a new sheet and name it **Context Filter**.

2. Double click on **Product Name** and **Sales**. This will give you the **Sales** of all the **Products**. Sort it descending by using the sort icons on the tool bar.

Since there are so many Products, it will be good if we just make a subset of **Top 10 Products by Sales**.

3. Place **Product Name** on the **Filters** shelf. From the popup dialog, navigate to **Top** and select the following options

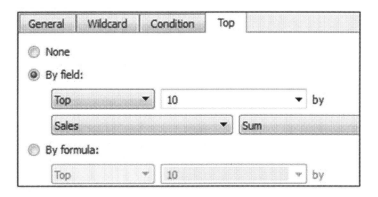

The Resulting chart will be like the one below

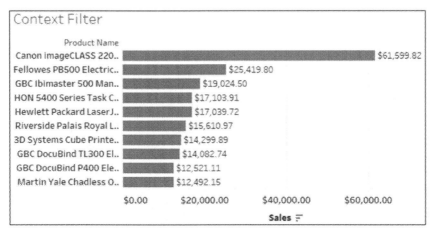

This creates a sub-set of only the **Top 10 Products**.
4. On the filter shelf, use Pull down menu on **Product Name** and select **Add to Context**. It will display in Grey color which indicates that it is a context filter.

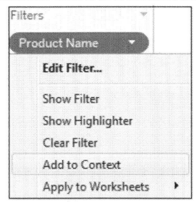

7. Now drop **Category** field on the Filter shelf and select "Technology". This filter will act on the subset created by the **Product Name context filter**.

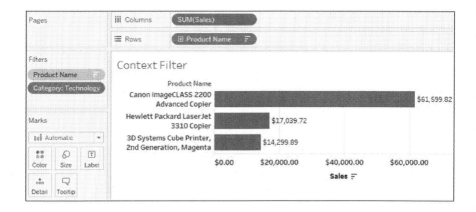

Parameters

- Parameters make the visualizations dynamic and interactive. Parameters acts like a variable that changes the hard-coded value to the user-input.
- A Parameter is not a filter but can be used in Filters.
- Parameters can also be used in the calculated fields.
- On the view canvas, the Parameter is always a single select.
- Parameters are useful only if connected to the data. This is done by using Parameter in a calculation.

Download sample workbook - http://tabsoft.co/2oZKhl6
Exercise - Using Parameter in a filter

Use parameters to find the Top N of Sales by Sub-category
    1. Use OnlyData.twb and save it as Chapter6-Parameters.
    2. Double click on **Sales** and **Sub-category**. You will get a bar chart.
Sort bar chart in descending order by using the Sort

options ![sort icons] from the tool bar.
    3. From Dimensions, drop **Sub-Category** to **Filters** shelf.

On the Filter ([Sub-Category] box, navigate to **Top**.
Make the following selections to **Create a new parameter**

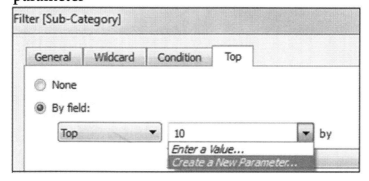

4. On **Create Parameter** box, make the following settings

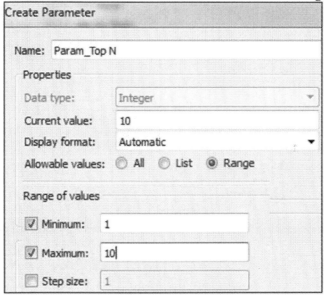

5. This will create a parameter called **Param_Top N**. The parameter definition will be displayed in the **Parameters** section in the data pane, below the **Measures**.
Since this is a numeric parameter, it will be displayed as a slider on the view canvas. The slider can be used to for user input.

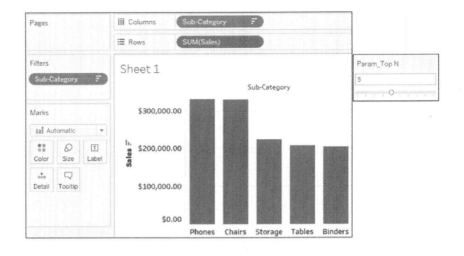

Exercise - Using Parameter in a calculated field

1. Use the same workbook Chapter6-Parameters and create a new sheet, **Parameter in Calculated field**.
2. Right click on **Segment** and select **Create/Parameter**.
3. It is already filled in the required boxes. You can always change them, if needed. Click ok.

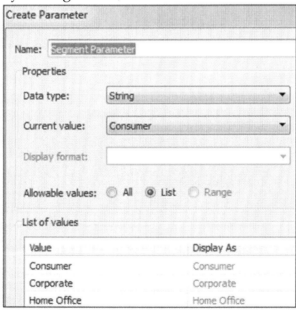

4. Right click on any empty space on the **Measures** section and Create/ Calculated field.

5. Name calculated field as "**Discount By Segment**" and use the following expression

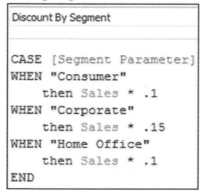

```
Discount By Segment


CASE [Segment Parameter]
WHEN "Consumer"
     then Sales * .1
WHEN "Corporate"
     then Sales * .15
WHEN "Home Office"
     then Sales * .1
END
```

6. Double click on **Region, Discount By Segment** and **Sales**. Tableau will create a Table.
7. On the data pane, right click on the parameter **Segment Parameter** and select "Show Parameter Control"

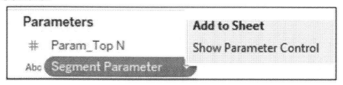

```
Parameters                    Add to Sheet
  #  Param_Top N             Show Parameter Control
Abc  Segment Parameter
```

8. In the view canvas you will get a Table and parameter control for selection. You can change the display of the parameter from the pull down menu. Remember that a Parameter can only be single select.

Pages		
	Columns	Measure Names
	Rows	Region

Filters
- Measure Names

Marks
- Automatic

Color	Size	Text
Detail	Tooltip	

- Measure Values

Measure Values
- SUM(Discount By Se...)
- SUM(Sales)

Parameter in Calculated field

Region	Discount By Segment	Sales
CZ	50,124	$501,239.89
EZ	67,878	$678,781.24
SZ	39,172	$391,721.91
WZ	72,546	$725,457.82

Segment Parameter
- ⦿ Consumer
- ○ Corporate
- ○ Home Office

7
Sorting

Sorting involves arranging data elements in the view in a specific order.

Sorting Basics

- Sorting can be ascending or descending. Sorting can be on dimensions or measures.
- Sorting can be done by clicking on the sorting button on the axis of a chart.
- Pill sorting option is available only for dimensions.
- Color legends also can be sorted manually.
- Sorting can be manual or computed.

Manual Sorting

Manual sorting can be performed by using the sort icons on the tool bar or by manually dragging the items within the view.

Download sample workbook - http://tabsoft.co/2p2Mtcl

Exercise

1. Open OnlyData.twb and save as Chapter7-Sorting.

2. Rename Sheet1 as **Manual Sorting**.

Double click on **Region** and **Sales**. Use **Show Me** to get a bar chart.

3. Change the **Default property** of **Sales** to display numbers in Millions.

3. Use the Sort icons ⊞ ⊞ on the tool bar to sort ascending or descending.

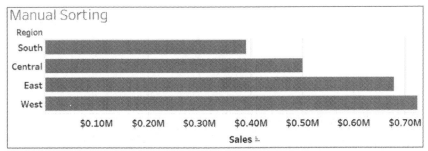

4. Sorting can also be performed by dragging and dropping the **Region** values to the desired position. Click on East and drag it over to Central.

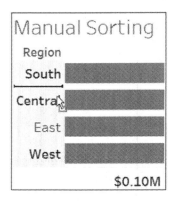

Computed Sorting

Unlike manual sorting, computed sorting follows some rules.

- Computed sort is applied to the Dimensions or discreet values. Except for the Filter shelf, a discrete field placed on any other shelf can be sorted.
- Dimensions on a worksheet can be sorted independent of other dimensions.
- Sort is computed based on the value of the filters and Sets in the view.
- Sorting of a dimension depends on the location on the view. If a field is placed on the Columns, values in that column will be sorted. If a field is placed in the Color shelf, the color will be sorted.
- Sort is computed across the entire table.
- Sorting does not break the dimension hierarchy.

Exercise

1. Use Chapter7-Sorting. Create a new sheet and name it **Computed Sort_Table**.

2. Place **Order Date** on the Columns and **Region** on the rows.

3. Place **Profit** on the **Text** under **Marks.**

This will create a table, sorted in Alphabetical order of Region.

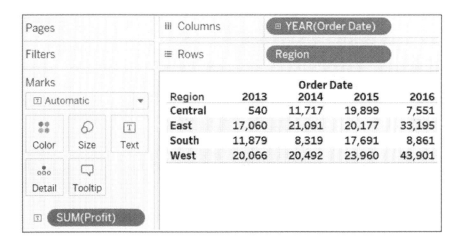

		Order Date		
Region	2013	2014	2015	2016
Central	540	11,717	19,899	7,551
East	17,060	21,091	20,177	33,195
South	11,879	8,319	17,691	8,861
West	20,066	20,492	23,960	43,901

4. Click on Year pill and select the **Sort** option

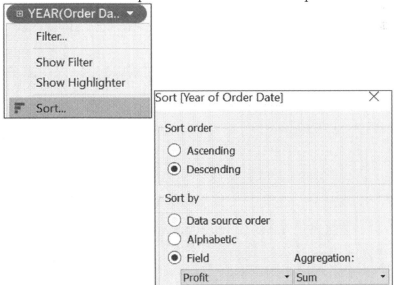

5. Select similar Sort for Region.

6. Navigate to **Menu-Analysis** and add Column and Row Grand Totals.

The resulting sorted table will look like the one below. Region West is on the Top because it has maximum Sales across all the Years.

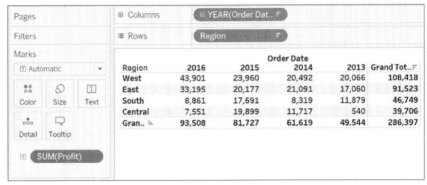

Region	2016	2015	Order Date 2014	2013	Grand Tot...
West	43,901	23,960	20,492	20,066	108,418
East	33,195	20,177	21,091	17,060	91,523
South	8,861	17,691	8,319	11,879	46,749
Central	7,551	19,899	11,717	540	39,706
Gran..	93,508	81,727	61,619	49,544	286,397

Nested Sort

Nested sort is helpful when visualization involves multiple dimensions and a measure, and normal way of sorting does not work.

Why Nested Sort

Consider the following scenario,

1. Use Chapter7-Sorting. Create a new sheet and name it **Why Nested Sort**.

2. Place **Region** and **Segment** on the Rows and **Profit** on the Columns.

3. If you sort this chart by descending, you will not get the right order. You would expect it to Sort by Region and Segment but Tableau will not do that. It has instead sorted by Sum(Profit) by Segment.

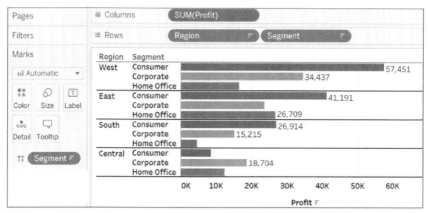

This issue can be resolved by creating a combined field.

Exercise - Nested sorting using Combined field

1. Create a **Duplicate** of the previous sheet and name it **Nested Sort**.

2. From the data section, crtl + click **Region** and **Segment** and select **Create/Combined Field**.

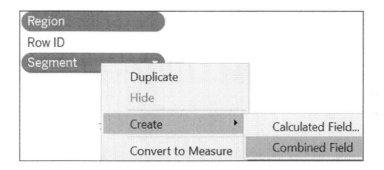

This will create a combined field in the Dimensions.

Abc Region & Segment (Combined)

3. Place this combined field in between Region and Segment on the **Rows**.

4. In the view, right click on the combined field column and uncheck **Show Header**

5. Now sort the chart by descending from the sort buttons in the tool bar. You can see that the sorting is now done by Region and Segment.

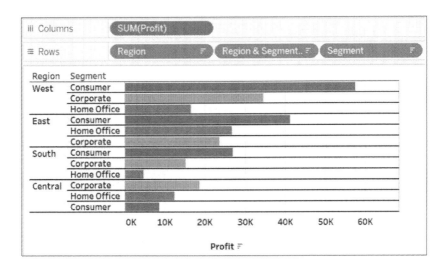

8
Groups and Sets

Groups are created to combine or group the values of a source column into a separate field. Grouped dimensions can be used as any other field.

Groups Basics

 • Groups can be created to correct data anomalies, for example USA, US can be grouped into United States.

 • Groups can also be used to combine dimension values, for example Tennis racquet, Ball can be grouped as Sports Goods.

 • A dimension can be a part of only one Group.

 • Groups cannot be combined to create another groups.

 • In Tableau 10, Groups can be used in calculated fields. In Tableau 9, this feature was not present.

 • Groups can be a part of the hierarchy.

Download sample workbook - http://tabsoft.co/2qxM7e2
Exercise - Creating Groups

1. Open OnlyData and save as Chapter8-GroupsSets Rename Sheet1 as **Groups**.
2. Double click on **Sub-Category** and **Sales**. Tableau will create a bar chart or select one from **Show Me**.
3. Ctrl + click the headers for **Binders**, **Bookcases**, and **Envelopes**. A small toolbar box will popup. Click on the **Clip icon** for **Group Members**.

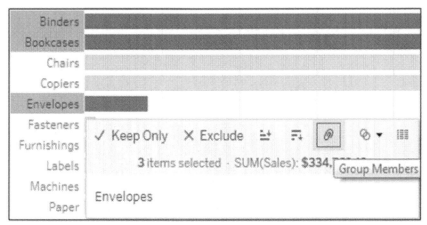

This will create a new dimension for **Sub-Category (group)**. This name can be changed by using Alias or rename.

4. The chart will now display a single bar for Sum (Sales) across **Binders, Bookcases, Copiers,** and **Envelopes**. The dimension on the Rows is also changed to the new group dimension Sub-Category (Group). This group is also created as a column in the **Dimensions** section.

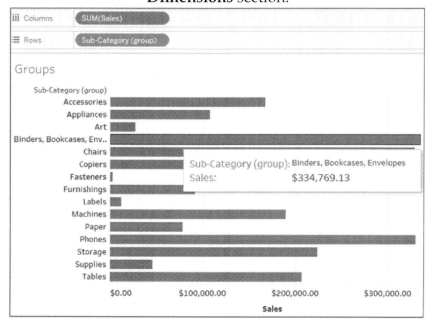

Exercise - Creating Groups using different Dimensions

In the above example, we grouped the values in the same Dimension field - Sub-Category. We can also group values from different dimensions.

1. Create a new sheet and name it "Grouping different dimensions".

2. Double click on **Sales** and **Quantity** from the Measures and **Region** and **Sub-Category** from the Dimensions. Alternatively, you can Ctrl + Click all these fields and select a chart from the Show Me.

This will create a scatter chart, with Region on the Shape and Sub-Category on Color.

3. Highlight over the desired Marks and click on Group in the pop-up tool bar.

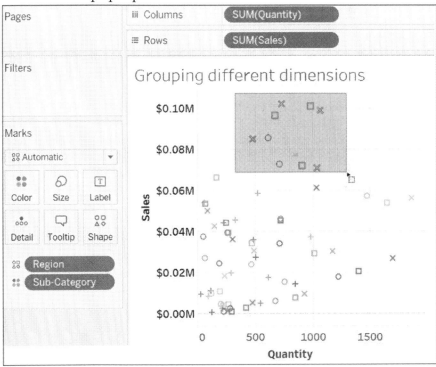

When you click on the group, you will have the option to keep all the dimensions in the Group or the specific dimensions.

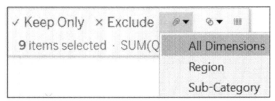

Select **All Dimensions**, this will create a **Group** with **Region** and **Sub-Category** dimensions.

⌀ Region & Sub-Category (group)

Exercise - Creating Group from the Data window

1. Create a new sheet "Groups in Data window".
2. Right click on **Sub-Category**, navigate to **Create/Group**.
Ctrl and click on **Accessories**, **Art** and **Machines** and click **Group**.

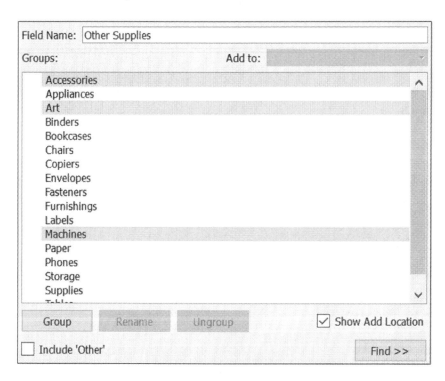

Name this group as "Other Supplies"

3. To add a new member to the Group, use the **Add to**: option in the above box.

4. This group can be used as any other field in the visualization by placing it on the Rows or Column shelves.

5. Once Group is on the shelf, use the pull down menu – Include 'Other' to create "Other" group to include items which are not in the "Other Supplies" group.

Use Sales and Other Supplies with "Include Other" option to create a table

Groups in Data window	
Other Supplies	
Accessories, Art, Ma..	**Other**
$0.38M	$1.91M

Sets

Sets are created to get a Sub-set of data.

Sets Basics

> • Sets work like any other field and are based on conditions. Sets create kind of a temporary table or filtered results.
>
> • A Set can be created by using the fields in the view. Sets can be used in calculated fields and can be used to create another set.
>
> • Sets can be a part of the hierarchy.
>
> • The same dimension field can be in multiple sets.
>
> • Sets once created will appear at the bottom of the data window.
>
> • Sets show up with different icons, depending on how they are created.
>
> • When a Set is placed on the Filter, it will show In/Out option. This indicates the values that fall within the Set or outside the set.
>
> • Two Sets based on the same dimension can be combined.
>
> • Actions in a dashboard will create Sets automatically.
>
> • User filter, used for Publish workbook will have user filter Set icon.

Exercise – Create Set for Top Sales by Sub-Category and Region

> 1. Use Chapter8-GroupsSets. Create new Sheet and name it **Sets**.
> 2. Double click on Measures - **Sales**, **Quantity** and Dimensions - **Sub-Category** and **Region**.
> 3. Highlight **Marks** on the view and select **Create Set** by clicking on the overlapping circles from the tool bar.

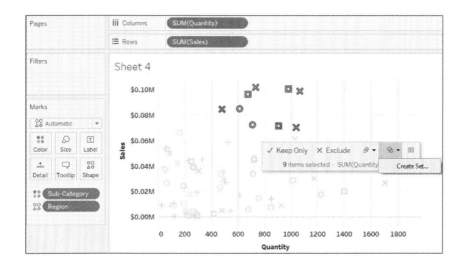

4. Name this Set "Highest Sales by Region and Sub-Category".

Create Set	
Name: Highest Sales by Region and Sub-Category	
Members (9 total):	
Region	Sub-Category
Central	Chairs
Central	Phones
East	Chairs
East	Phones
East	Storage
West	Chairs
West	Phones
West	Storage
West	Tables

This Set will appear below the Measures in the data pane.

Exercise - Using Sets as Filter

Sets once created can be used in the visualization to get meaningful results.

1. Create a new sheet and name it **Using Sets as Filter**. Ctrl click on **Sales, Quantity, Region** and **Sub-category**. If you don't get a scatter plot, use scatter plot from Show Me.

2. This will display Sales and Quantity by Region and Sub-category.

But we are interested only in seeing the result for "Highest Sales by Region and Sub-Category".

3. Drop the **Set** (created in the previous exercise) on the **Filters** shelf. Right click on the **Set** filter and select **Show Filter**. Set filter will show options of **All, In, Out**. Use this filter to see the result for the Set of Highest Sales or values which are outside this set.

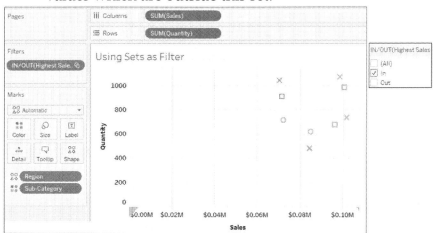

Exercise - Creating Dynamic Sets

Dynamic Set changes when the data updates.

1. Use the same workbook and create a new sheet **Dynamic Sets**.

2. Right click on **Customer Name** and navigate to **Create/Set**.

3. In the Create Set box, navigate to **Condition** tab and do the following settings

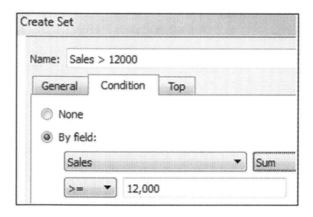

4. Now create a visualization, double click **Customer Name** and **Sales**.

Since we are interested in seeing the Sales > 12,000, place Set Sales > 12000 on the **Color** shelf.

5. On the visualization, you will get the bars satisfying this condition in blue and the rest grey.

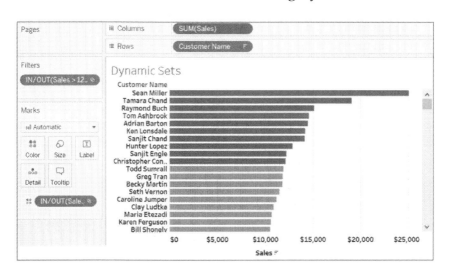

Combine Fields

Two dimension fields can be combined to create a cross-product of the two fields. When a combined field is used in the view, it displays the data for the combination of both the fields.

Exercise

   1. Create a new sheet and name it **Combined**.

   2. On **Dimensions**, ctrl + click on **Region** and **Segment**, right click and select **Create/Combined Field**.

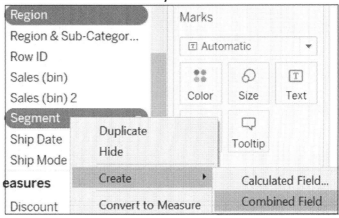

This will create a new field in Dimensions as "Segment & Region (Combined)".

Segment & Region (Combined)

3. Double click on **Segment & Region (Combined)** and **Sales** to create a Table. Notice number of rows in the table is 12 as we have 4 Regions and 3 Segments.

Segment & Region (Combined)	
Consumer, Central	$252,031
Consumer, East	$350,908
Consumer, South	$195,581
Consumer, West	$362,881
Corporate, Central	$157,996
Corporate, East	$200,409
Corporate, South	$121,886
Corporate, West	$225,855
Home Office, Central	$91,213
Home Office, East	$127,464
Home Office, South	$74,255
Home Office, West	$136,722

9
Formatting

Tableau provides formatting options to enhance the visual experience. Formatting helps in keeping the same look and feel of the visualization across the workbook.

Formatting makes the visualization more appealing and useful. It draws attention to the data and helps in analysis.

Formatting Basics

- The Formatting pane is contextual; it displays items based on the items selected.
- Marks can be used to provide **Color**, **Size**, **Label**, **Detail** and **Tooltip**.
- Marks type can be changed to change the data representation in the charts.

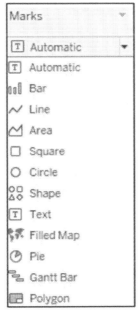

- Filters on the view canvas can be formatted from the pull down menu.

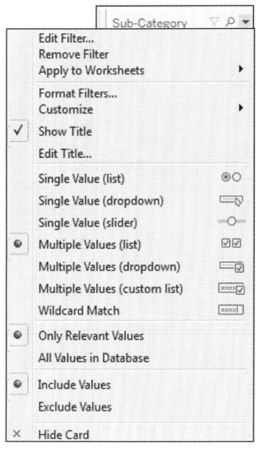

Formatting can be applied to any object on a sheet. Formatting menu can be invoked from **Main Menu – Formatting** or by **right-clicking on the object.**
Following formatting options are available,

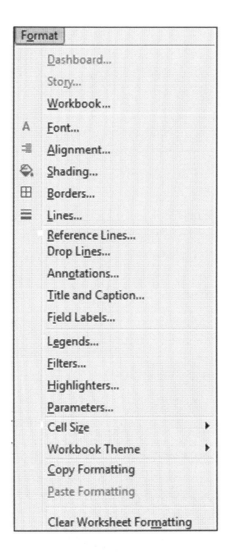

- If a field is placed on the Label, then the label will get displayed in the view. It is equivalent to clicking 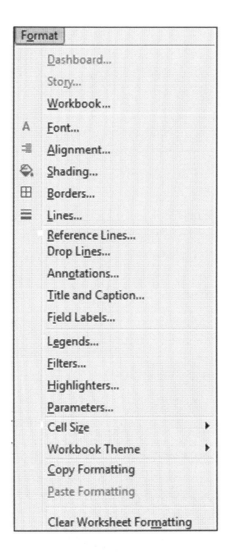 on the tool bar. A Label can also be formatted by simply clicking on it.
- As a best practice, Formatting should be defined at the higher level, such as Workbook and then lower level such as Sheet. The formatting configured at the Workbook level, will flow to all the lower levels such as Worksheets and Objects.

- Workbook theme can be changed from default to Modern or Classic.
- Colors play an important role in visualization. In a dashboard, keep consistent colors for the data elements, for e.g. if Regions are depicted in a specific colors in one sheet, same color combination for Region should be followed in all the sheets.
- Discrete/Dimension columns are displayed in unique colors. Measures/Continuous columns are displayed in color range.
- Use muted colors so that the user attention is on the data and not on the colors. Overuse of colors should be avoided.
- Use **Tooltip** to provide more information on the data point. Tooltip can also be formatted in different colors and fonts.

Download sample workbook - http://tabsoft.co/2pzvYpe
Exercise

Specify Formatting at the Workbook level. This will reflect changes in all the sheets in the workbook.

1. Open OnlyData.twb and save as Chapter9-Formatting.
2. Create two sheets. In **Sheet1**, use **Sub-Category** and **Sales**.
   In **Sheet 2**, use **Region** and **Profit**.
   This is to see how formatting is effecting the visualization.
3. Navigate to Main Menu - **Format/Workbook**.
   A formatting screen to specify **Fonts** will open up over the Data section.

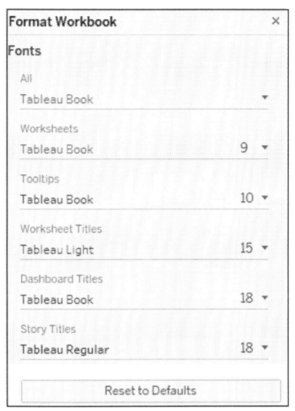

The options displayed in the above screen-shot are for **Fonts** at different levels.

4. Use the drop-down menu next to **All** to specify the **Font type** and **Font color** at different levels. All formatting settings can also be customized for the specific object such as Sheet or chart.

For this example, use **Arial** and **Orange**.
Observe the changes in your visualization.

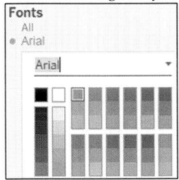

Your visualization on **Sheet1** will look like, the one below. Hover over Sub-category - Bookcases, even Tooltip formatting has changed.
Check **Sheet 2,** it will reflect the same color and font.

Sheet 1

Sub-Category	
Accessories	$167,380.32
Appliances	$107,532.16
Art	$27,118.79
Binders	$203,412.73
Bookcases	$114,880.00
Chairs	$329,449.10
Copiers	$14...
Envelopes	$1...

Sub-Category: Bookcases
Sales: $114,880.00

5. On the formatting pane, Click on the drop-down next to **Worksheets** and change the color to **Black.**
Observe changes in the Sheets.
Tooltip still shows in orange as we made changes only at the worksheet level.
6. On the formatting pane, click on the drop-down/pull-down next to **Tooltips** and change the color to dark blue and bold. See how changes reflect in your visualization.
7. Similarly, you can make changes to **Worksheets Titles**, **Dashboard Titles** and **Story Titles**.
Any changes made at this level will reflect in the entire workbook.

❖ To undo all the formatting changes, just click on **Reset to Defaults** at the bottom of the formatting dialogue box.

Exercise
Specify Formatting at the **WorkSheet** level

1. Navigate to **Sheet 1** and from the Main-menu, **click on Format/Font**. The following dialogue box will get displayed over the Data pane.

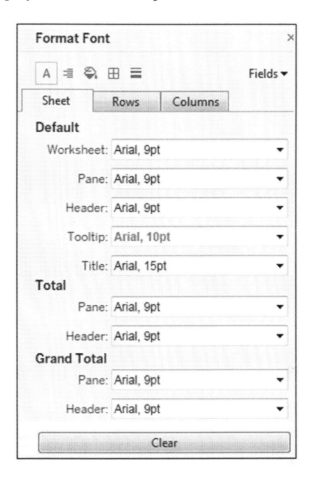

Using this dialogue box, you can make changes to **Fonts**, **Alignment**, **Shading**, **Grid** and **Lines**.
2. Notice that the changes made in the previous exercise at the workbook level are still present.
 Now make changes to the fonts, sizes etc. and see the changes. Observe that the changes made in Sheet 1 are not reflected in Sheet 2.
To clear your formatting changes anytime, click **Clear** at the bottom of the formatting pane.

3. Formatting can also be done by right-clicking on the header or value on the view/visualization and select **Format**

5. **Size** on Mark type can also be used to increase or decrease the size of the shapes or data elements on the view.

6. To change the number format of a Measure, navigate to **Measures** in the data section Right click on any measure, such as **Sales, Default Properties, and Number format.**

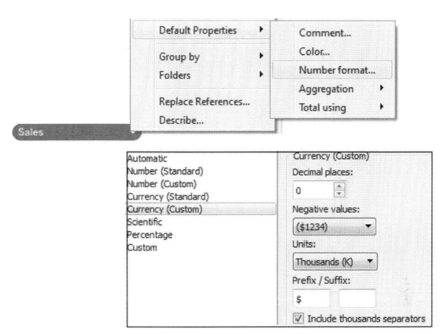

7. Formatting done in one sheet, can be copied to another sheet to maintain the consistency. This is done by right clicking on the source/Sheet and selecting **Copy formatting** then right clicking on the Target sheet and selecting **Paste formatting**.

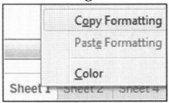

Copy and paste formatting will paste only the worksheet level formatting. Any formatting changes to view objects such as Marks, Color, size or Label are not copied.

How Colors work in Tableau

Colors help in presentation of data. Colors can be assigned to Dimensions or Measures.

- Color can be created by placing Dimensions or Measures on the Mark type **Color.**
- Dimensions are discreet. If a dimension field is placed on the **Color** shelf, a distinct colors are assigned to the data element.
- Measures are continuous in nature. When Measures are placed over the **Color**, a sequential color palette is generated.
- Colors can be edited by clicking on the color shelf and selecting **Edit Colors**.
- Colors can be assigned RGB or HTML code. To assign such codes - **Edit Colors** and double click on the color.
- Specifying color in the calculation will not assign colors, as it is just a measure. To get the color, the calculation should be placed on the Color shelf.

Exercise – Categorical vs Sequential colors

To understand colors, let us create a chart

1. Chapter9-Formatting and create a new sheet, **Categorical Colors**.

2. Place **Region** on the row and **Sales** on the Columns. This will create a bar chart.3. From the dimensions, place **Region** on the **Color**. This will create and display Region values in unique colors.

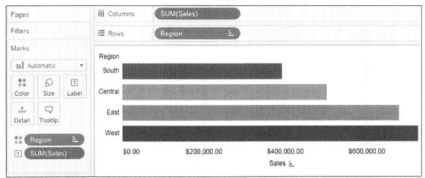

This color assignment can be changed by using **Edit Colors.** You can select a specific color or provide RGB or HTML codes.

4. Duplicate this Categorical Colors sheet and call it **Sequential Color**.

5. Now place Sales on the Color and replace Region from the color.

Since Sales is a measure and is continuous, bars in the chart will have just one color of varying intensity.

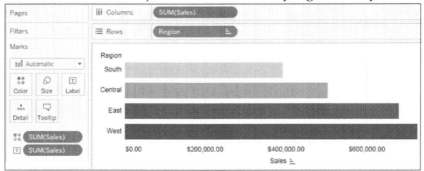

Creating Custom Color Palettes

Tableau desktop provides plenty of color palettes to assign colors to dimensions and measures used in Maps, Charts and Tables.

Tableau also allows the creation of Custom Palettes by modifying **Prefrences.tps** file. This file is located in My Tableau Repository folder.

Prefrences.tps file is a xml file and can be opened in any text editor, such as, notepad.

Tableau provide a template of the file.

```
<?xml version='1.0'?>
<workbook>
</workbook>
```

- ❖ Tableau does not support custom color palettes, therefore take backup of your workbooks before making any changes.
- ❖ In certain releases, Tableau introduces new Color Palettes and modifies/discontinues others. If you want to continue using the discontinued Color Palettes, edit Prefrences.tps to add the hex values for the palette.

Exercise
Creating custom categorical palette
A **Categorical** color palette contains unique colors that are assigned to discrete dimensions values. For example, if you use Region on the **Color,** you will get a distinct unique color for each Region.

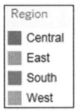

1. Navigate to your **My Tableau Repository** folder under **Documents** and open Prefrences.tps in notepad.
2. Type the following code. After the changes, the code should look like

```
<?xml version='1.0'?>
<workbook>
    <preferences>
        <color-palette name="Custom Categorical
Palette" type="regular" >
                <color>#eb912b</color>
                <color>#7099a5</color>
                <color>#c71f34</color>
                <color>#1d437d</color>
                <color>#e8762b</color>
                <color>#5b6591</color>
                <color>#59879b</color>
        </color-palette>
```

```
        </preferences>
</workbook>
```

❖ In the above code, **type = regular** identifies that this is a categorical palette.

3. Save and Close Prefrences.tps.
4. Close Tableau Desktop application.
5. Open Chapter9-Formatting.twbx.

Create a new sheet, drop a discrete dimension, like, Region on the **Color** Card. Click on Color card and choose **Edit Colors...**

Under **Select Color Palette,** at the bottom select your **Custom Categorical Palette.**

6. Click on **Assign Palette** to assign these custom colors.

Exercise

Creating custom Sequential Color palette

A **sequential** color palette is used for continuous fields like Measures. This color palette shows the same color in different intensity.

The changes in the Prefrences.tps will be similar, except for **Type** attribute. For Sequential palette, use **type="ordered-sequential"**

    1. Open Prefrences.tps and do the following changes

```xml
<?xml version='1.0'?>
<workbook>
    <preferences>
        <color-palette name="Custom Categorical
        Palette" type="regular" >
            <color>#eb912b</color>
            <color>#7099a5</color>
            <color>#c71f34</color>
            <color>#1d437d</color>
            <color>#e8762b</color>
            <color>#5b6591</color>
            <color>#59879b</color>
        </color-palette>

        <color-palette name=" Custom Sequential Palette"
        type="regular" >
            <color>#eb912b</color>
            <color>#eb9c42</color>
            <color>#ebad67</color>
            <color>#eabb86</color>
            <color>#eacba8</color>
            <color>#ebd8c2</color>
        </color-palette>
    </preferences>
</workbook>
```

Close Tableau desktop application and open Chapter9-Formatting again.

2. Create a new sheet and use **Sales** on the **Color. Edit Colors** and look for the **Custom Sequential Palette.** Click on **Assign Palette** to use the custom palette.

Highlighter

Highlighter is a new feature in Tableau 10. This new feature lets you highlight the specific data element in the view while maintaining the context of all the data in the view.

1. Use Chapter9-Formatting. Create a new Sheet Highlights.

2. Double click on State and Profit. This will create a Map with Profit for each Sate.

3. Drop **Customer Name** on the **Detail**. This will display, Profit by each Customer and State.

4. Now to Highlight Specific Customers and see in which State they do business, click on the Customer Name pill and select **Show Highlighter**.

This will display a **Highlight Customer Name** filter. Hover over the Customer name and it will Hightlight the Customer in different states.

10
Creating Maps

Maps help in plotting geographical locations around the globe. Tableau creates a Map based on the Latitude and Longitude of a geographical location such as Country or City. Any location on a Map, is indicated by a Latitude and Longitude.

Map Basics

- Tableau has internal database that contains common geographic fields.
- Tableau creates Latitude (generated) and Longitude (generated) fields for the identified geographical locations.
- Tableau automatically creates a Map for recognized locations. If Tableau does not contain the desired Latitude and Longitudes, you can define them in a database or a csv file.
  - This custom geocoding can be imported in the Tableau environment by navigating **main menu** to Map /Geocoding/ Import Custom Geocoding.
- A Location on a Map can be plotted as a point or mark to represent the entire area or polygon covering the area.
- Tableau contains many built-in polygon data or filled Maps for many geographic locations. It is also possible to provide your own polygon data to create custom polygon Maps.
- Apart from default Maps, Tableau has an option for Web Map service or WMS. Using WMS, you can upload your image and assign coordinates.
- Tableau automatically assigns geographical role to location fields. Fields having the geographical role assigned can be identified by a **globe symbol** next to them .

- Sometimes Tableau cannot recognize a field as a geographical location. For example, sometimes a Zipcode can be identified as number. In such instances, you can right click and assign a geographical role to the field.
- Geographical roles available in Tableau are

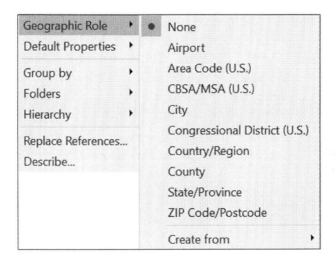

- Area code contains USA telephone area codes.
- CBSA/MSA is USA metropolitan Statistical Areas.
- City are worldwide cities with population more than 15,000.
- Congressional District are U.S. congressional districts.
- County/Region are worldwide countries.
- County represents counties of few countries such as the USA, France, Germany etc.
- State/Province represents worldwide states.
- Zip code/ Postalcode of selected countries are available

Download sample workbook - http://tabsoft.co/2p2SINj
Exercise - Creating a Map

1. Open OnlyData.twb and save as Chapter10-Maps.

2. Double click on **State** field and it will automatically be plotted on the Map of USA. Tableau automatically places **Longitude** and **Latitude** on the **Columns** and **Rows** shelves. **State** is placed on the detail on **Marks**.

3. Drag **City** and drop it on the Map. Now you have cities for each state.

These fields have created a Symbol Map. In **Symbol Maps**, locations are represented by circles in the Mark. Circle Map type can be changed to other Mark types such a shape or size.

4. You can drop **Region** to **Color** and **Profit** on the Map. The Map will show Profit in each State and City.

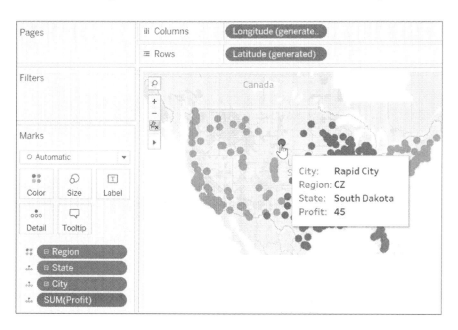

Symbol Map can be changed to **Filled Map**, by changing the Mark to **Filled**.

Filled Maps are not available for City geographical location.

5. Create a new sheet and name it **Filled Map**. Double click on **State**. This will create a Map. Change the Mark type to **Filled**. You will get a filled Map. Drag **Profit** to the color shelf.

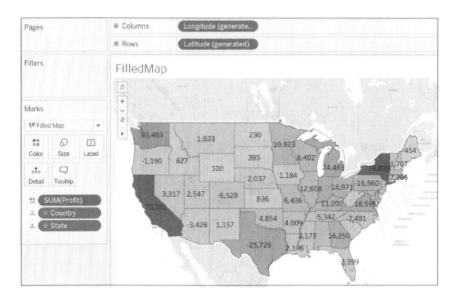

Map Layers

By default, Tableau Maps are in grey scale, this can be changed by using Map layers. **Map Layers** will help in enhancing the look of the map.

Navigate to Main Menu - Map/Map Layers

Explore different Background style – Normal, Light and Dark. Use **Washout** option to set the intensity of the background. Use **Map Layers** to display other features of the geographic location, like Land cover, coastline, Borders.
Tableau also provide predefined **Data layer** that show U.S. Census information.

```
┌─────────────────────────────────────┐
│ Map Layers                          │
│ Background                          │
│                                     │
│  Style:   │Light            ˅│      │
│  Washout:──────────█────────│48%│   │
│      ☐ Repeat Background            │
│ Map Layers                          │
│   ☑ Base                       ᨈ    │
│   ☑ Land Cover                      │
│   ☐ Coastline                       │
│     Streets and Highways            │
│   ☐ Light Country/Region Borders    │
│   ☐ Light Country/Region Names      │
│   ☑ Country/Region Borders          │
│   ☑ Country/Region Names            │
│   ☐ Light State/Province Borders ˅  │
│ Data Layer                          │
│                                     │
│  Layer:│Population            ˅│    │
│  By:   │State                 ˅│    │
│  Using:│▭ Blue-Green Sequential ˅│  │
└─────────────────────────────────────┘
```

Editing Unknown Locations

When a geographical location is placed on the view, Tableau
automatically creates the Map.

Sometimes at the bottom of the Map, you will notice **<number>
Unknown.** This happens because Tableau is unable to decide
where these locations exists.

Exercise

    1. Create a new sheet and name it **Edit locations-1**.

    2. Double click **City**. A symbol Map will be created. On
the bottom right of your screen, you will notice "**146
unknown**". This unknown shows that Tableau is unable
to decide the **State** of these cities. There may be same
cities in one or more States.

❖ If you are unable to reproduce this, drag out Country and State under the **Marks**.

3. This can be resolved in two ways,

One way is to drop **State** to the **Detail** card. This will correctly Map cities to the State.

Whenever such ambiguity of location occurs add the higher-level location in the location hierarchy.

Another way is explained in the section below.

More on resolving Unknown locations

1. Create a new sheet and call it **Edit Locations-2**. Double click in **City**. If the entire location hierarchy Country and State is coming with it, then drag out Country and State for right now.

2. When you see **146 unknown,** click on it and Tableau will prompt with a dialog box. Click on **Edit Locations**

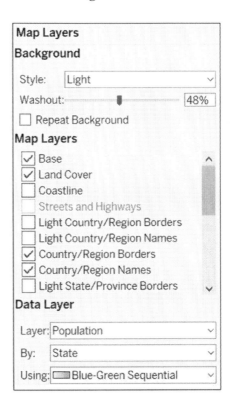

In the **Edit Locations** dialogue box, the first option is **Country/Region**.

This displays the country of the physical computer. In our case it is the USA. Also this is the only country available in this dataset.

The Second option is **State/Province**, click on the State/Province option and tell Tableau to use State from the source data field.

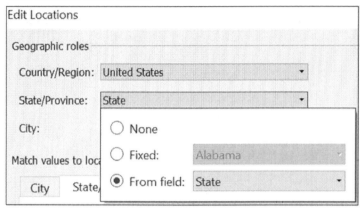

Notice that "unknowns" have gone.

3. If sometimes, the source data contains misspelled names of City or State, correct those by typing in the correct names in the **Matching location box.**

4. If in case, you have a location that is not being recognized by Tableau, you can manually enter the latitude and longitude of that location. Click on the Matching Location box and select "Enter a Latitude and Longitude".

This option will appear only for the problematic locations.

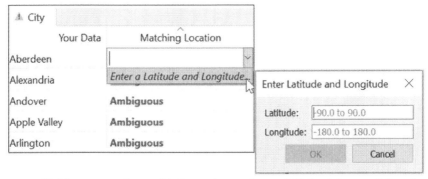

5. You can also edit locations, from Main Menu- **Map/ Edit Locations**.

Building Custom Territories

A new feature in Tableau 10 enables you to add your own custom territories.
This can be done in two ways,

- Using Groups
- Designate a territory field to a geographic role

Exercise

Due to recent structure changes, your organization has come up with new Sales territory. You need to plot these territories on the Map and display the total Sales in these territories.

1. Use Chapter10-Maps.
2. Create a new sheet and name it Custom Territory.
3. Double click on **State** and **Sales** from the data pane. This will create a Map with Sales for different states. Since USA is the only Country, remove country from the Marks.
5. Highlight the States which you want to include in your custom Territory and click on the **Group** icon to create a group.

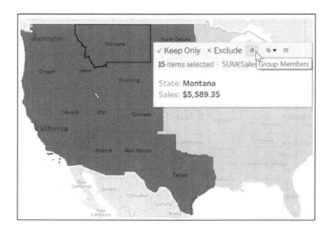

A group  field will be created in Dimensions. In the same way, high-light other states and create other territory groups. These States will also be added to the **State(group)**. It will also display as a legend.

State (group)

▢ Alabama, Arkansas, Florida and 14 more
▢ Arizona, California, Colorado and 13 more
▢ District of Columbia, Maine, Maryland and 10..
▢ Other

❖ The grey color **Other** are the States not in the group. These states can be filtered, renamed or added to the existing groups by editing the State(group).

Now remove the **State** from the mark. This will display the customized territories and Sales in those territories.

Designate a territory field to a geographic role

1. Create a new sheet and name it DesignateTerritoryField.

2. Double click on **State** and **Sales**. Drag out/remove Country from the Marks. Place **Region** on the **Color**.

Notice, even though Map is divided in separate Regions, Sales is still for specific State.

3. On the dimension, right-click on the **Region** and select as follows

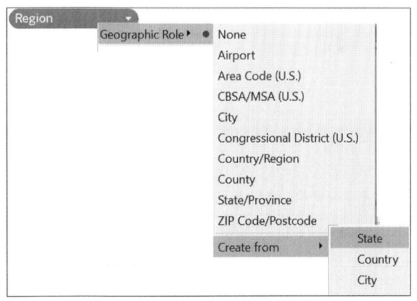

Drag out the **State** from the Mark. You will get total Sales per Region.

11
Creating Visualizations

Visualizations provide an insight into raw data and help executives in making informed decisions. A Visualization is a combination of Tables, Charts and Maps. Based on the data fields selected, Tableau automatically applies best practices and suggests the visualization type to be used.

So far, you have created a few visualizations. In this chapter we will look into it in more detail.

Visualizations basics
- Visualization is a visual representation of data. In Tableau desktop, **Show Me** suggests the best visualization based on the dimensions and measures selected.
- Visualizations are created on a **Worksheet.** You can create only one visualization per Worksheet. **Dashboards** are a combination of one or many Sheets. **Story** contains one or more Dashboards or Worksheets.
- Visualization should be created to answer business queries.
- Usually on a screen, data is read from left to right. Place important content on the left.
- Use muted colors, since loud colors distract the users. The objective of the dashboard should be to draw attention to the data.

Download sample workbook - http://tabsoft.co/2oRLmQC

Text Table

Text table is a great way to view Numeric data.
There are different ways to represent data in charts but sometimes it is more readable to display the same data in the table.
Text table requires one or more dimensions and measures. Create a Table to display Sales by Segment for each of the Years.

1. Open OnlyData.twb and save as Chapter11-Charts. Rename sheet 1 to **Tables**.
2. Place **Order Date** on **Columns**, **Segment** on **Rows** and **Sales** on **Marks - Text**. This will create a simple Text Table.
3. Navigate to **Main Menu - Analysis** and navigate to **Totals**. Select "**Show Row Grand Totals**" and **Show Column Grand Totals**".

| Segment | | Order Date | | | |
	2011	2012	2013	2014	Grand Total
Consumer	$266,096.81	$266,535.93	$296,295.54	$332,473.06	$1,161,401.35
Corporate	$128,434.87	$128,757.31	$206,942.95	$242,011.23	$706,146.37
Home Office	$89,715.81	$75,239.27	$105,235.34	$159,462.73	$429,653.15
Grand Total	$484,247.50	$470,532.51	$608,473.83	$733,947.02	$2,297,200.86

Heat Maps

In a Heat Map, data is represented in terms of Colors. It provides a quick visual summary of the data.

1. Right click on the Sheet **Tables** and select **Duplicate**. Name this new sheet **Heat Maps**.

2. From Show Me, click on the second icon for Heat **Maps**. This will convert Table to Heat Maps. Adjust the size, and you will see a chart with Boxes according to the size of the Sales in each Segment and Year.

3. **Ctrl + click** Sum (Sales) and place it on the **Color**. Since Sales is a measure and is continuous, it will show continuous color palette.

4. Click on the **Color** card and click on **Edit Colors**. From the **Palette** drop down, select **Red-Green Diverging**.

You will get a Heat Maps colored in Green and Red based on the amount of Sales in each Segment and Year.

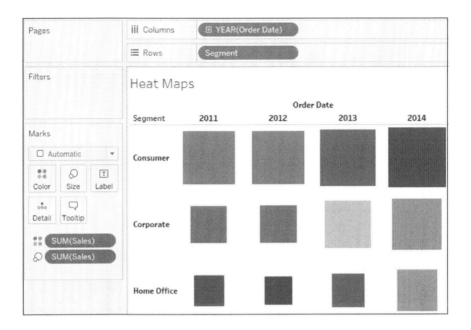

This chart can also be converted to **Highlights table**, which is similar but presents Text in colors based on the data.

Highlight Table is also present in **Show Me**.

Segment	Order Date			
	2011	2012	2013	2014
Consumer	$266,096.81	$266,535.93	$296,295.54	$332,473.06
Corporate	$128,434.87	$128,757.31	$206,942.95	$242,011.23
Home Office	$89,715.81	$75,239.27	$105,235.34	$159,462.73

Maps with calculated colors/Dual – axis Map

Maps provide analysis based on geographic locations. For geographic fields, Tableau creates a Map automatically.
In the following Map, we will plot Sales by Region and State. Sales will be shown in circles. The size of the circle will show the amount of Sales in a particular state.

1. Create a new sheet and name it "Map".
2. From the Dimensions, double click on **States** and **Sales**. Change Mark type to **Filled Map**.
   This will display the Map in one color.
3. Place **Region** on the **Color**. This will create color for the Region on the Map.
   Click on the **Color** and select **Edit Colors**. Check the colors assigned to Region, you can change if you want.
4. On **Measures**, click on **Sales** and create a calculated field and name it "**Sales Color**". Use the following calculation
   if Sum([Sales]) > 100000 then "Green"
   ELSEIF   Sum ([Sales]) < 100000 and Sum ([Sales]) >= 50000
   Then "Yellow"
   ELSEIF Sum ([Sales]) < 50000 then "Red"
   END
5. Click on **Latitude** on the **Rows** shelf. Crtl + click and make a copy of it.

   This will give two Maps one at the top and one at the bottom.
6. On the **Rows**, click on the second **Latitude.** Now place calculated field "**Sales Color**" from Measures to **Color card.**

7. With the second Latitude still selected on the Rows, change the **Mark type** to **Circle**. This will change points on the bottom Map to circles.

8. Navigate to **Rows** and click on the pill of the second Latitude and from the pull down menu, select **Dual axis**. This will overlay the second Map on top of the first Map. You will see one Map with filled states and circles.

9. Click on the second latitude again and from the Mark Type, increase the **Size** of the circles. Click on Size and adjust the size.

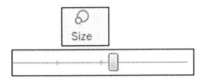

10. If Colors on the circles do not get displayed as expected, click second **Latitude**, click on the **Color** and **Edit Colors...** select the right colors from the palette.

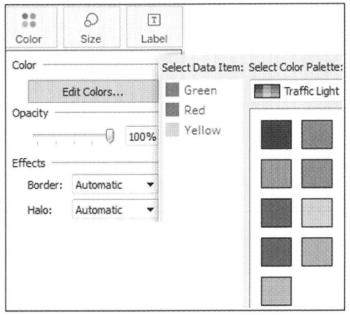

After all the color and formatting changes, your Map will look like

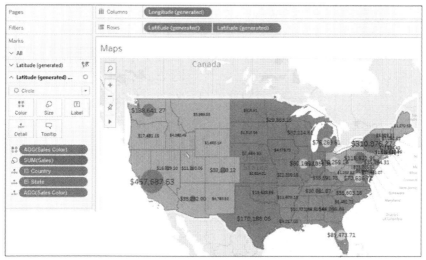

11. Hover over the Map and see if the desired **Tooltip** is displayed. Tooltip can also be modified and formatted as mentioned in the previous chapter.

12. Drop **Region** and **State** filter by right clicking on the fields and select **Show Filter**.

Pie Chart

Pie chart is useful to show different slices of a Category as percentage of the total.

Pie charts are useful if the number of slices is less.

1. Create a new sheet and name it "Pie Chart".
2. Place **Segment** on **Columns** and **Profit** on the **Rows**.
3. Click on the pill for Sum(Profit) and navigate to **Quick Table Calculation**.

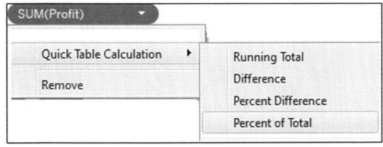

4. Click on **Show Me** and select **Pie chart**

5. This will create a Pie chart. Click on the label symbol on the tool bar to display the percentages on the slices.

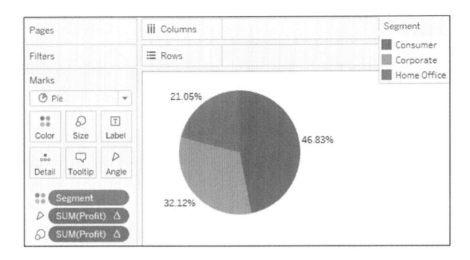

Donut Chart

Doughnut chart is a slight variation of a pie chart. In addition to colors, pie chart also displays the angle.

1. Create a new sheet **Donut chart.**
2. Place **Number of Records** twice on the **Rows.** You can use any measure or calculation just to get the shape of the Donut.
3. By default the aggregation will be Sum(Number of Records), you can change it to **Attribute** too.
4. Click on the second **Number of Records** on the **Rows** and select **Dual Axis.**
5. From the **Mark Type**, select **Pie** for both the measures. They will both show in the same color.
6. Click first **Number of Records** on the **Rows** and **Edit Color** to be **Orange.** Click on the second **Number of Records** and change its color to **White.**
7. If you don't see the donut, increase the **size** from the Size card.

8. Click on the first **Number of Records** on the **Rows**
   a. Drop **Segment** on the **Color** card. The Donut will show in different colors.
   b. Drop **Profit** on the Label.
   c. Click on the **Profit** on the label to create a **Quick Table Calculation** - Percent of Total
9. Click on the second **Number of Records** on the **Rows**
   a. Hide the labels by clicking on ☐T on the tool bar
   b. From the Measures, drop **Profit** on the **Label** card.
10. In case you don't see all the labels, Click on the first **Number of Records** on the **Rows** and click ☐T on the tool bar

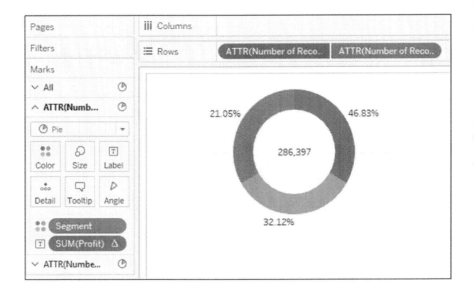

Bar and Combination Chart

Bar Charts provide data representation of discrete elements or unique categories.

Bars can be displayed vertically or horizontally. On a Bar chart, discrete Categories are displayed on the axis, with length of the Bars showing the value of each of the Category.

Bars can be **grouped/stacked**, where the length of the bar represents the value derived from the combination of the discrete categories.

> 1. Use Chapter10-Charts. Create a new sheet **Bar_Combo**.
> 2. Double click on **Sales** and **Segment**.
> Create a bar chart that will give Sales by Segments. Sort it in descending order.
> Drop **Segment** on **Color** to get the distinct color.
> 3. On a bar chart, you will have a measure on one axis and Dimension on another.

Combination/Combo Chart

4. Double click on **Quantity.** This will create another chart as only one measure can be displayed on a Bar graph.

6. Click on **Quantity** on the Rows and from the drop-down menu select **Dual Axis.**

7. This will change the visualization. Click on **Sales** on the Rows and make sure the Mark Type is **Bar**. Click on **Quantity** on the Rows, and change Mark Type to **Line.**

8. Create a filter for **Segment** by using b.

This kind of chart which combines a **Bar** and a **Line** to display two measures is called a **Combination Chart.**

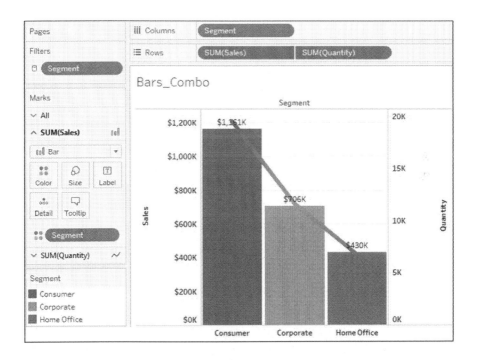

Stack Bar Chart

Stack chart is created to display the part of the whole. Stack chart is a kind of Bar chart, with each bar divided into different Categories.

1. Create a new sheet and call it "Stack chart".
2. Double click on **Order Date** and **Sales**. Create a bar chart. If the Bar chart is not displayed automatically, select one from **Show Me**.
3. Place **Category** on the **Color**. This will create a stack chart. It will show in each Year, the Sales from each of the Category.
4. Click on Mark label icon ⊤ on the tool bar to display the labels on the bar.

Treemaps

Treemaps are used to display hierarchical/tree data. The visualization is displayed in rectangles, where the size of the rectangle is ordered by the **measure** selected.

You can drill down to the lower level of the data.

Treemap is more suited to display large amounts of hierarchical data in a limited space.

1. Use Chapter11-Charts. Create a new sheet and name it Treemap.
2. Double click on **State** and **Sales**. Since State is a geographic field, Tableau will automatically create a Map. Change map to the Treemap, by selecting from **Show Me**.
3. Remove Country under the Mark as we have just one Country "United States" in the data and it is not adding any value.
4. This creates a treemap for the **Location** hierarchy. The size of the rectangles displays the Sales in each state. It is visually easier to compare the Sales in different States.
5. Drop **Region** on the **Color** and it will display States in different Regions.

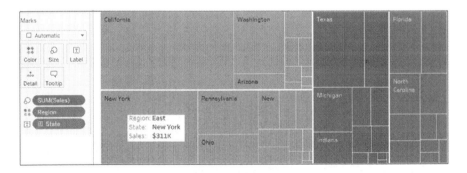

You can click on the + symbol next to **State** to drill down to the lower level of the hierarchy like City and Zip.

Line Chart

Line charts are useful to show trends over time.

1. Create a new sheet and call it **Line Chart**.

Place **Order Date** on the Columns and **Sales** on the Row.

Select Lines ⊞ from **Show Me**.

2. Place **Category** on the **Color**. On the Columns, drill down to Month.

3. From Dimensions, right click on **Order Date** and select **Show Filter**. Select only 2014 from the filter. Line chart will display, Sales of each Category by different Months in 2014.

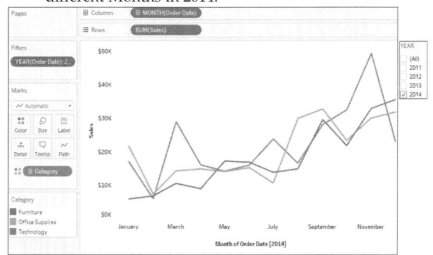

❖ In the screen-shot above, months are not being displayed in the correct order, for e.g. Feb is not displayed after January. This is because when the size of the chart is reduced, Tableau automatically hides a few months. If this chart is set to "Entire View" you will be able to see all the months.

Area Chart

Area chart is a combination of a line chart and a stack chart. It fills the area between the lines with colors to show the overall amount by different categories over time.

1. Create a duplicate of the previous Line Chart and call it **Area Chart**.

2. From Mark Type, select **Area Chart**. It will convert the Line chart into an Area Chart.

Area chart is similar to Stacked chart. It is more useful when it can show the Percent of the total.

3. On the **Rows**, click on Sum(Sales) and select **Quick Table Calculation – Percent of Total**

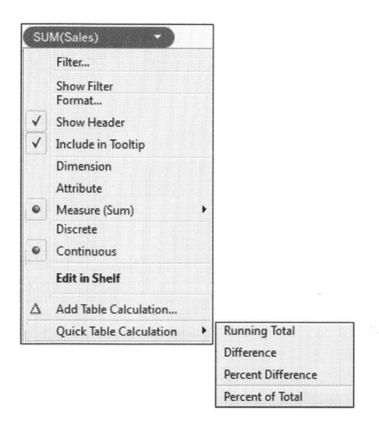

The resulting chart will appear like

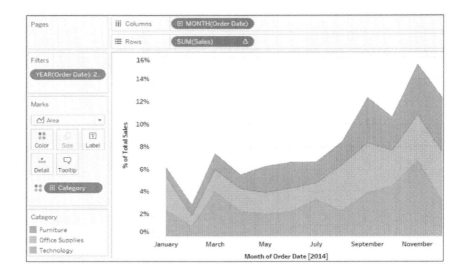

Scatter Plot

Scatter Plot is used to display the relationship between two measures.

1. Create a new sheet and call it **Scatter Plot**.
2. Place **Sales** on Columns and **Profit** on the Rows. Tableau will automatically create a scatter chart. It displays Total Sales and Total Profit.
3. Place **Region** on the **Shape** and **Color**. Now you have Sales and Profit by each Region.
4. Place Sub-Category on the **Detail**, it will display Sales and Profit by each Region and Sub-category.

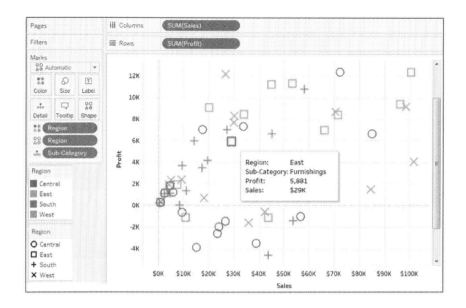

Box and Whisker Plots

Box and Whisker plot provides a quick glance at the distribution of data statistically.

Given a data set, it displays the **Median, Lower Quartile (Q1), Upper Quartile (Q3), Interquartile range, highest observation** and **Lowest Observation**.

It displays Quartiles in **Box** and **Whiskers**.

Box represents inter-quartile range i.e. distance between the Upper quartile and Lower Quartile.

Whiskers represents Q1, Q3, Lowest and Highest Quartile.

> 1. Create a new sheet and call it **Box Plot**. Place **Sub-Category** on the **Columns** and Profit on the **Label**. This will give you a table.
>
> 2. From **Show Me** select Box-Whisker plot ╫╫╫╫

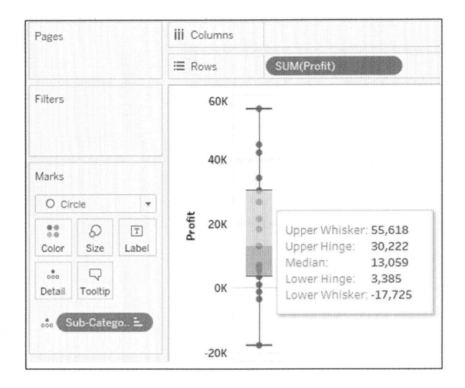

❖ Understanding Median, Q1 and Q3

Median, Q1, Q3 divide sorted dataset into 4 equal parts.
Where,

Median is the middle or 50% position of the count of numbers in the list.

Q1 is 25% of the count of numbers

Q3 is 75% of the count of numbers in the list.

- Duplicate the sheet **Box Plot**. From **Show Me** convert it into a Table by using **Show Me**.

There are 17 numbers in the table.

Median is (n+1)/2 i.e. (17 +1)/2 = 9

In the list of numbers the number on 9th position is 13,059. Therefore, Median is 13,059

Q1 is 25% of 17 i.e. 4.25 or the 5th position. Therefore, Q1 or Lower hinge is 3,385

Q3 is 75% of 17 i.e. 12.75 or the 13th position. Therefore, Q3 or Upper hinge is 30,222

Bullet Chart

Bullet chart is similar to Bar chart and is used to replace data presented in gauge or meter charts but with more information. Bullet chart is used to compare a primary measure against a constant or dynamic measure.

For e.g., to see if the primary measure meets the threshold target or is falls within the range of 60% and 80%.

1. Use Chapter11-Charts and create a new sheet **Bullet Chart**.
2. Place **Sub-Category** on the **Rows** and **Sales** on the **Columns**. This will create a bar chart.
3. Right click on the **x-axis** and select **Add Reference Line**

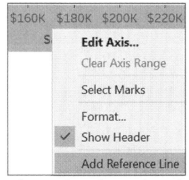

In the next dialogue box, select the options for **Line** and set the other values as below

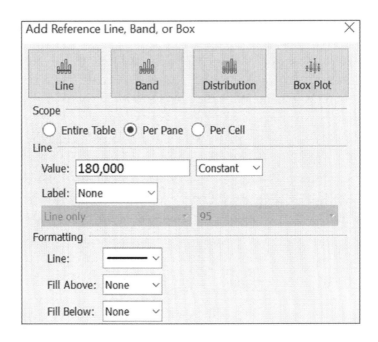

❖ We have entered a constant Value of 180,000. You can also have this target dynamic if it exists in your dataset.

The above settings will create a **Target line** in your bar chart.

Add 60% 80% shaded area,
Again right click on the **x-axis** and select **Add Reference Line.**
This time select **Distribution** and **Per Pane**.
In the **Value** drop-down select the same constant value 180,000 which we specified in the earlier reference line.

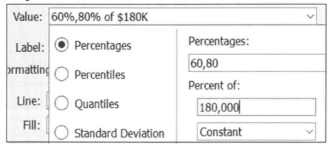

This will create the shaded areas of 60% 80% of 180,000.
After doing all the changes, your dialogue box as below

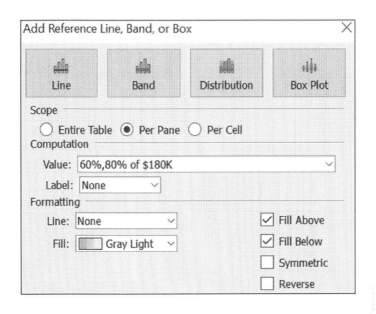

The resulting bullet chart will look like the one below.

The **dark vertical line** shows the Target Sales of 180,000 and the shaded dark and light grey areas show 60% and 80% threshold. From this chart, you can clearly see which Sub-Categories meet the Target, which are above or below the Target. The Grey areas show which Sub-Category sales fall within 60% and 80% range.

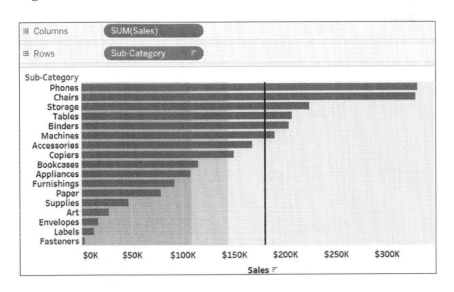

Histogram

A Histogram shows the distribution of a measure in a dataset. It displays how many times a particular measures occurs in the dataset.

It is similar to a bar chart, except that bar graphs are used to plot the discrete data and Histogram is used to plot the continuous measure.

Histograms create equal size **bins** or group of equal-sized numeric ranges. This bin can be modified to create a customized range.

To create a histogram you need just one measure.

1. Use Chapter11-Charts. Create a new sheet **Histogram**.
2. Double click **Quantity** and from **Show Me** select Histogram 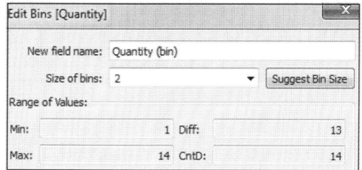.
3. When the histogram chart is created, tableau will automatically create a bin, named **Quantity (bin)** under **Dimensions**.

    By default, Tableau has given a **Size of** 1.77 to **bins** but this bin size can be changed or you can create a bin as a calculated field.
4. For this exercise, change it to **2**. Right click on the **Quantity (bin)** and change the **Size of bins** to 2. Tableau will automatically set the other attributes

Edit Bins [Quantity]			X
New field name:	Quantity (bin)		
Size of bins:	2	▼	Suggest Bin Size
Range of Values:			
Min:		1	Diff:	13
Max:		14	CntD:	14

In the resulting chart, the bar represents the count (Quantity) in each of these bins.

5. The values on the x-axis will automatically start from 0 and an extra bin is created. You can change it to start from 1 and end at 16.
   Right-click on the x-axis and **Edit the Axis**

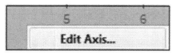

Change **Range** from **Automatic** to **Fixed**

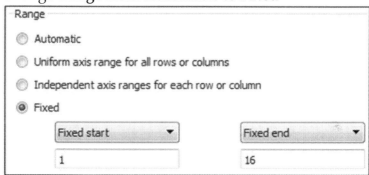

6. Drop **Category** on the Color. The resulting histogram will show you Count (Quantity) in each of the bin/s and Quantity sold in each of the Category.

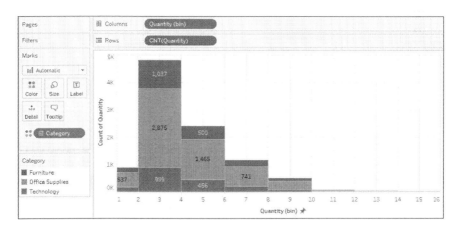

Clustering

Clustering is a new feature in Tableau 10. Clustering groups related data elements together.

Clustering feature is available in the **Analytics pane** on Tableau desktop. Clustering is similar to creating groups. Tableau uses K-means algorithm to create a cluster.

1. Create a new sheet and name it **Clustering**.
2. Double click on **Sales** and **Profit** to create a scatter chart. Place **Customer Name** on the **Detail**. This will give you Sales and Profit by each customer.
3. Navigate to **Analytics** tab. This tab is next to the **Data** tab on the left.
4. Click on **Cluster** and place on the view.

This will display the variables used in creating the cluster and Number of Clusters/Groups. By default, Number of Cluster is **Automatic** but this number can be changed. It also displays the color legend of the Clusters.

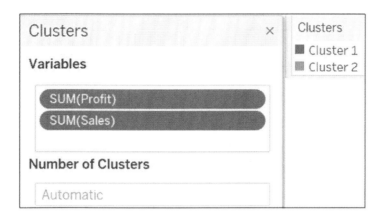

To learn how Clusters are created, right on **Clusters** on Marks and select **Describe clusters**.

Clusters can be added as a field to Dimensions and can be used in other visualizations.

12
Dashboards and Visual Story

Dashboards are similar to automobile dashboards where all the useful information is present at a glance. In Tableau, Dashboard is a collection of Worksheets. Dashboards can be used to compare information on different sheets.

Dashboards are created like any other sheet in Tableau Desktop.

Dashboard Basics
Dashboards follow similar principles as visualizations.

- Dashboards should be designed for a specific screen size or device, such as desktop, laptop or mobile devices.
- Dashboard in Tableau is a collection of one or multiple sheets. As a best practice, related sheets should be displayed in a dashboard.
- Dashboards should not be over cluttered. Too many sheets will distract the users.
- Muted and consistent colors should be used.
- As the human eye scans the screen from left to right, all important information should be placed on the left of the screen.
- On a dashboard, a sheet can act as a filter for other sheets. This filter should be placed on the top-left corner.
- **Actions** should be used to create interactive dashboards.

Dashboard Designing Options

- On a Dashboard, the Left pane offers different options for Device Preview, Screen Size, Sheets to be displayed on the dashboards and formatting.
- Tableau 10 has a new feature **Device Preview**. It shows different Device types and Models. This will help you see how your dashboard will get displayed on different devices.

- Dashboards should be designed for a specific user group screen size. **Size** Option provides with all the options.
- **Sheets** section provides a list of sheets in the workbook that can be included in the dashboard.

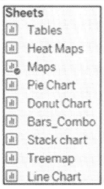

- **Objects** section provides
  - **Horizontal** and **Vertical** layout containers where sheets and filters can be displayed.
  - Option to put image, text or webpage on the dashboard.
  - Dashboard objects can be **Tiled** or **Floating**. **Tiled** objects are displayed in a non-overlapping grid. **Floating** objects can be placed anywhere on the screen and can be layered on top of other objects.

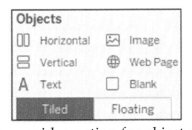

- The **Layout** tab provides option for object placement on the screen. This is helpful when the **Floating** option is selected. Custom **x** and **y** position and object size can be provided.
  The Layout tab also provide information on all the objects placed in the dashboard and layout containers.

Download sample workbook - http://tabsoft.co/2ppFixC
Exercise - Creating first Dashboard – Sales Map

1. Save Chapter11-Charts created in previous chapter as Chpater12-DashboardsStory.
2. This workbook will have all the worksheets you created in the previous section.
3. From the bottom of your screen, either click on the dashboard icon ![icons] or right click on any sheet and select **New Dashboard**. Name this dashboard as "Db_SalesMap".
4. From the left pane, select the **Dashboard** size as **Automatic**

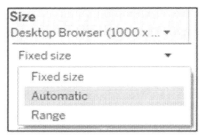

5. Double click on the **Maps** sheet from the left. You can also use the layout containers for object placement.

6. Dashboard object can have filters as specified in the sheet or data elements used in the dashboard. Since Filters were already specified on the Map, they will get displayed automatically.

7. Otherwise, click on the **Map** and from the pull down menu on the top-right corner, select the filters needed for this dashboard.

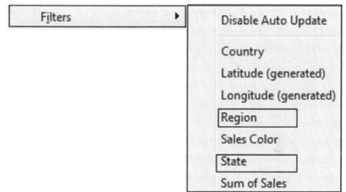

8. Select **Region** and **State**. Since there are large number of States, from the **State filter** pull down menu, select Multiple Values (dropdown) option.

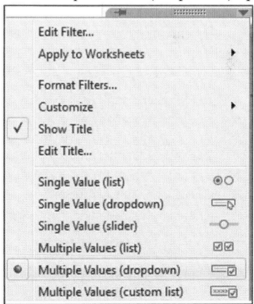

7. Right now, State filter is not dependent on the Region filter and shows all the States irrespective of

8. the Region selected. To make it dependent, from the State Pull down menu select **Only relevant values**.

Only Relevant Values

9. Your dashboard should look like the one below. The map is displayed for Region – Central and West.

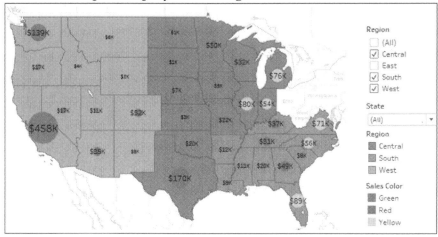

Exercise - Creating Second Dashboard – SalesBySegment

1. To create a new dashboard, from the bottom of the screen- click on the **New Dashboard** button. Name this dashboard as Db_SalesBySegment
2. From the list of dashboards on the left, double click on **Heat Maps, Bar_Combo** and **Tables** sheet. They will all be tiled on the screen. If you want to make them floating, select the floating option.
   If the **Segment filter** does not appear, you can use the pull down menu from Bars_Combo to display it.
3. From the Segment filter - pull down menu, select **All Using This data Source**

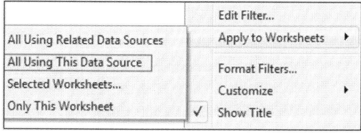

This will make sure that the Segment filter will work with all the Sheets/Charts simultaneously.
Your dashboard will look the following with Filter applied to all 3 dashboards.

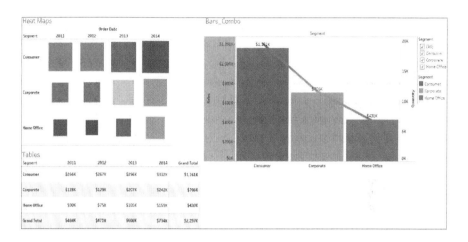

Actions

In Tableau, **Actions** provide interactivity between the sheets. Actions are also be used to link to other webpages and worksheets.

In the above dashboard, Db_SalesBySegment, Sheets can act like a filter.

1. Navigate to Heat Maps in the above dashboard, from the pull down menu, select **Use As filter**

> **Use as Filter**

2. Now click on the Segment or the rectangle boxes on the Heat Map and notice that it is behaving like a filter for other sheets.

Actions Explained

With the above dashboard still open, navigate to main Menu – Dashboard/Actions

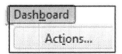

Action – **Filter** 1 is already created. This Action has been created since we changed Heat Maps to filter.
Select the Action and click on **Edit**.

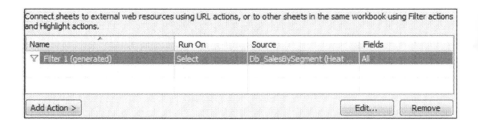

Action contains the following

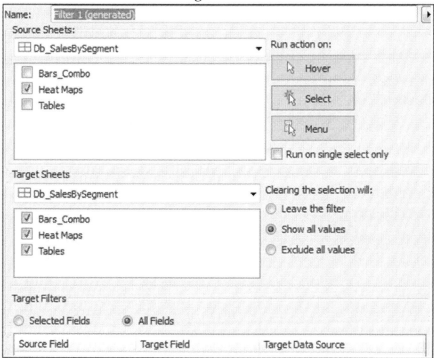

❖ Actions can also be added from the menu
Dashboard/Actions.

Types of Actions
There are 3 types of Actions,

- **Filter**, the one we saw above, to filter other sheets in the dashboard.
- **Highlight** Actions highlights the Marks on the chart.
- **Url** Actions is used to link to a webpage or link to other reports.

Exercise – Create a dashboard Overall Sales
1. Create a new dashboard and name it Db_OverallSales.
2. Double click on Stackchart, Treemap, Area Chart and Donut chart sheets.
3. Select the Stack chart to be used as a filter.

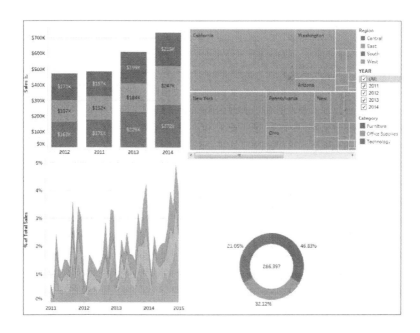

Story

A Story is a collection of dashboards and/or worksheets that are arranged in a sequence to provide information about business or a measure.

Story is created just like a dashboard or sheet

There can be more than one story in a workbook.
The Story environment looks similar to Dashboard,
The Left-pane displays the Sheets and Dashboards available in the workbook. It also provides options for sizing the stories.

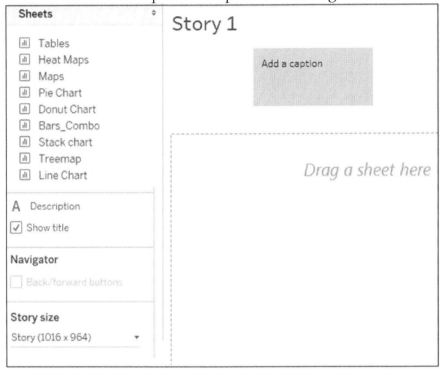

Exercise - Create Sales story of the Organization

1. Use the same workbook Chapter11_DashboardStory.
2. The Story is created like any other sheet in dashboard. You can use icons  or right click on any sheet and select New Story.
3. Rename this Story as **Sales Story** and drag it all the way to the left so that it becomes the first sheet in your workbook.
4. Click on the **Sales Story**, from the bottom left, change the size of the Story to **Automatic**.
5. Click on **Add a Caption** box and enter text as "Sales by Location". Place Db_SalesMap in the center of the canvas in "Drag a Sheet here". If at any time, you have to navigate to the sheet, click on the small arrow at the left on the sheet.

> Db_SalesMap

6. Click on **New Blank Point** box on the top and add caption as "Sales by Segment". Drag Db_SalesBy Segment to the center of the canvas.
7. Again click on **New Blank Point** and add caption as "Overall Sales". Drag Db_OverallSales to the center of the canvas.
8. We can add a sheet also on the story. Click on the New Blank Point and add caption "Actual vs Target" and add Bullet Chart.

This creates a Sales Story, which provides the overall analysis of Sales in an Organization.

Click on the presentation icon ⬚ on the tool bar. The Story will look like the one below

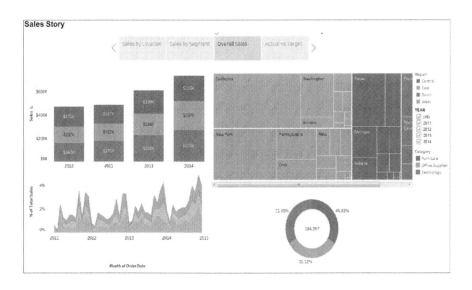

13
Server Deployment

There are multiple ways a user can view Tableau visualization application.

> • If user has Tableau Desktop license, user can view workbook on the Tableau desktop.
> • Tableau reader can also be used to view the application. Tableau reader is a free download from Tableau.com and accepts twbx file.
> • Tableau dashboards can be deployed on the Server. A server url is used to view the dashboards. Visualizations on the server can be secured.

Tableau Server Basics

- Tableau Server is a central repository for users, data sources, sheets and dashboards.
- Authorized users can view dashboards using the server url. No installation required on user's machine.
- Server can be used to
  - Refresh data extracts - TDE files
  - Publish and download data sources
  - To publish and view twbx and twb files
  - Secure sheets and dashboards
- Users can be created in Tableau Server manually or can be imported from Active directory server.
- Each user is assigned a role based on his organization structure. User can be a part of a group.
- On Tableau server, sheets and dashboards are organized in **Projects**. There can be multiple Projects and each project can have multiple sheets and

- dashboards. These projects can be viewed only by authorized users.
- Sheets and Dashboards are deployed on the Server via Tableau Desktop.

Tableau Installation

If you don't have licensed version of Tableau Server, download a two-week trial version from
https://www.tableau.com/products/server/download

Once you download and install Tableau server, you can access it by using the url http://yourmachine-name:80

❖ If you are installing Server on your local machine, select the option for **local authentication.**

Create Users on Tableau Server

1. Login to Tableau Server. If it is on your local machine, then type **Localhost** on your browser, it will popup Tableau Server login screen.
   Login with the Administrator credentials, you have setup during installation.

- ❖ In Tableau, users can be added from an Active directory, can be imported from a csv file and/or can be created manually. In the trial version, you will not see the option of adding the users from an Active directory.
2. Manually create the users according to the **People** sheet in Sample – Superstore.xls. Following users can be created

Person
Anna Andreadi
Chuck Magee
Kelly Williams
Cassandra Brandow

To create these users, click on the **Users** Tab from the top navigation bar on the Tableau Server and select **Add Users/ New User**.

- ❖ To create a Username, I followed *First-Initial of first name and last name*
- ❖ For password, I used *First name (capitalized the first letter) 123 i.e. Anna123 will be the password for the first user.*
  You can create users in whatever way you want.

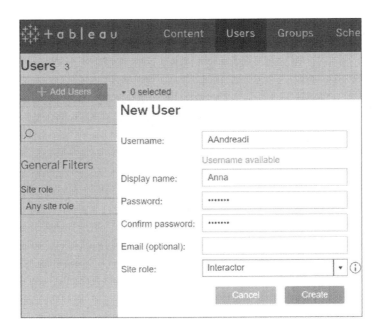

Specify the **Site role** as **Interactor**. This user can interact with the dashboard.

Different roles can be assigned to the user such as Interactor, Publisher etc.

Create remaining users also in the same way - CMagee, KWilliams, CBrandow

❖ In this section, following userid's and passwords are created:

AAndreadi/ Anna123
CMagee/Chuck123
KWilliams/Kelly123
CBrandow/Cassandra123

Create Groups

Groups are a way of organizing your dashboards. Business specific Groups can be created. Users are assigned to these groups.

Groups will help in implementing security. While publishing the Tableau views, you can make sure which Groups are authorized to view the specific dashboards.

1. On the Tableau server, click on the **Groups** tab and select **Add Groups**. Create a new group called **Sales 1**.

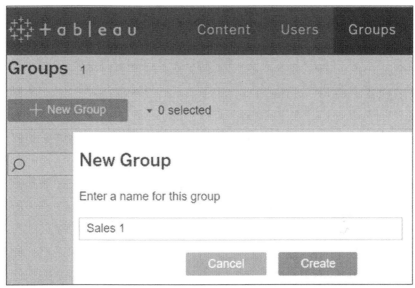

Create Groups Sales 2 and Sales 3 in the similar fashion.

❖ **All Users** group is created by default by Tableau and all users are added to that group.
Adding Users to the Groups
Navigate to that **Users** Tab. Check Anna Andreadi and change her Group Membership to **Sales 1**

In the similar fashion, add
- Cassandra Brandow to Sales 1
- Chuck Magee to Sales 2
- Kelly Williams to Sales 3

Create Projects

Projects contain business specific views or dashboards. Security can be applied to Projects as well, so that only authorized users can see a specific Project.

1. On the Tableau Server, navigate to **Content** tab from the top navigation bar.
Two Projects - Default and Tableau Samples get created with installation.
2. Click on **New Project** and enter the name of the Project. For this exercise, say **Project: Sales1.**
This Project has 0 workbooks, 0 Views and 0 Data sources.
3. In the similar fashion, create **Project: Sales2**

Publishing data sources on the Server

In Tableau, data sources can be published to the server so that other power-users can download them from the server and create their own dashboards.

1. Launch Tableau desktop and open Chapter12_DashboardsStory you worked in the last chapter.
2. Navigate to any worksheet and right click on the Data source **Orders(Sample – Super Store)**

This will open up a server connect dialogue box

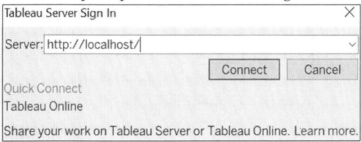

Specify your server url here. Once you click on **Connect**, you will have to provide your server userid and password.

After successful connection to the server, you will see a dialogue box **Publish Data Source to Tableau Server**.

- Provide the name of the Project
- Provide the name of the Data source, if you want to rename the data source while publishing
- In case of publishing an extract/TDE, specify the Data refresh schedule
- Click **Edit** next to the permissions and specify what kind of permissions you want to give and to what Groups.
- In this example, **All Users** is given permission to connect to the data source.

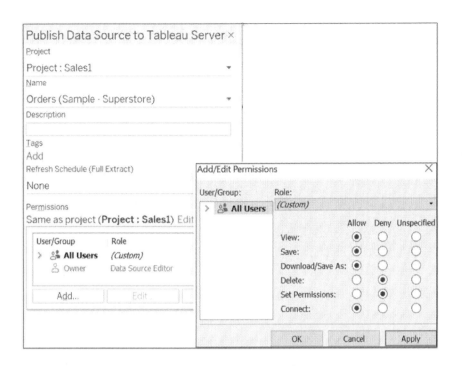

After applying all the settings, hit **Publish**
If data source is published successfully, you will get a
message

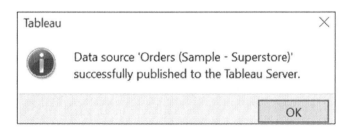

❖ To verify login to your Tableau server and check the
   Data Source tab.

Publishing visualizations on the Server

You can publish specific dashboards, sheets and stories to the Tableau Server.

1. Launch Tableau Desktop and Open Chapter12_DashboardsStory.

From the main -menu, navigate to **Server** and select **Publish Workbook**. You may have to connect to the server, if you are not already connected.

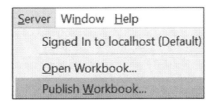

2. Views will be published to specific **Project**, select a Project and name the published workbook.

Under sheets, you have the option to publish **Only the dashboard** or **All the sheets** or specific sheets. In this example, I will publish, one dashboard and 2 sheets.

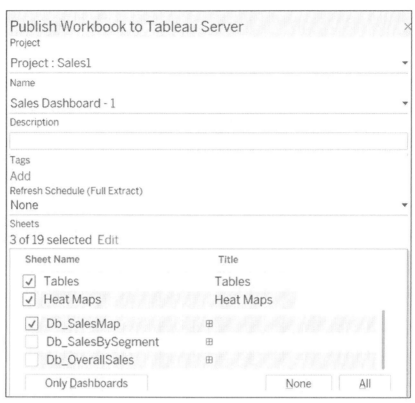

Give permission to Group **Sales 1** to view the dashboard. Leave rest options as default and publish the workbook.

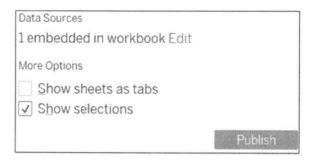

Once the workbook is published successfully, Tableau server will be launched and a message will be displayed

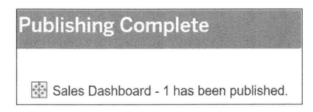

Sales Dashboard - 1 has been published.

On the server, you can see 3 views published.

3. In the similar fashion, publish other sheets and dashboards and assign them to a different Project. In the permissions select User/Group Sales 2

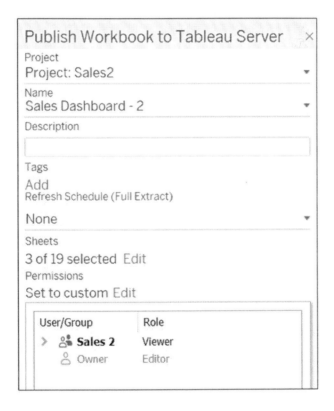

Securing Project on the Server

1. Login to Tableau Server as Administrator.

2. On **Content**, locate the **Project: Sales1** which you created in the previous exercise. You have published 3 views to this Project.

3. Hover over the Project:Sales1 box and click on the **...** in the right corner and select **Permissions**

On Tableau, all Projects are by default assigned to **All Users** group. Change "All Users" group permission to **Denied.**

On the same screen, from the options below, select **Add a user or group rule** and select user group **Sales 1**.

Change the permission of **Sales 1** to **Viewer**. The users in Group **Sales 1** will have viewer permission on the Project.

Securing Views on the Server

1. Login to Tableau Server as Administrator.

2. From the **Project**, go to a view. Hover over the view and click on **...** and select Permissions.

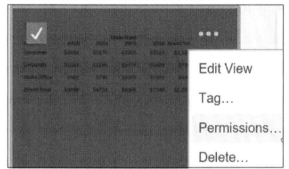

3. On Tableau Server, all views are assigned to **All Users** group. Change the permissions of **All Users**. Select **Denied** from the drop down.

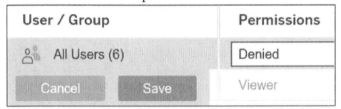

Sales 1 group will have Viewer permissions.

Verifying the security

1. Login to Tableau server as one of the user AAndreadi/ Anna123

This user can see only the dashboards assigned to her

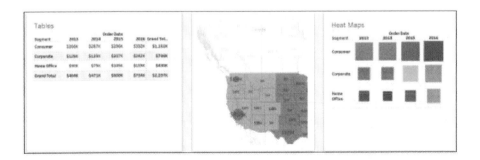

Index

About The Author

AUTHOR NAME is Chandraish Sinha
Find out more at amazon.com/author/ChandraishSinha
Or visit www.LearnTableauPublic.com

Can I Ask A Favor?
If you enjoyed this book, found it useful or otherwise then I'd
really appreciate it if you would post a short review on
Amazon. I do read all the reviews personally so that I can
continually write what people are wanting.
Thanks for your support!

Made in the USA
Columbia, SC
10 November 2019